SAKE BOOK

松崎　晴雄　著

日本酒　ガイドブック
《英語対訳つき》

What is Japanese SAKE?

日本酒とは ——その定義——

　日本酒は酒税法により、造り方や原料がきちんと定められている。酒税法では「清酒」と呼び、定められた条件を満たした、アルコール分が22度未満のものとなる。条件をわかりやすく説明すると、米、米麹、水を原料として発酵させて、濾したものだ。そのほか、原料に、清酒を搾ったあとに残る酒かす、醸造アルコール、糖類、酸味料など定められたものも使えるが、その重量の合計は、米と米麹の重量の半分を超えないことが条件。つまり日本酒とは、あくまで米と米麹を主原料に使い、発酵させて、最後に濾すという工程を経て造られるのが特徴の、醸造酒といえる。

How to make sake and its materials are defined by the Japanese Liquor Tax Act. Under the law,'Seishu' means what satisfies prescribed conditions by it and it must have an alcoholic strength of less than 22% volume. To put it plainly, it is fermented from rice, koji and water and then pressed. Some other ingredients such as sakekasu (strained lees of seishu), brewers alcohol, saccharides, acidifier and so on, can be used to it, but the gross weight of them must not go over a half of that of rice and koji. In other words, sake is the brewed beverage that is made by fermenting and pressing, the main materials of which are only rice and koji.

the SAKE BOOK

日本酒 ガイドブック

CONTENTS

Chapter 1

TYPES OF SAKE AND THE BREWING
日本酒の種類と作り方

Chapter 2

ALL ABOUT SAKE
日本酒大全

Chapter 3

HOW TO ENJOY SAKE
日本酒の楽しみ方

Chapter 4

LET'S GO TO IZAKAYA
居酒屋へ行く

the SAKE BOOK

日本酒 ガイドブック

CONTENTS

Chapter 5

RESTAURANTS SERVING SAKE IN TOKYO
東京で日本酒が飲める店

※本文中に表示されている価格（メーカー希望小売価格）は税抜表示が基本です。（2018 年 6 月現在）

The history of SAKE
日本酒の歴史

　日本酒がいつの時代から造られたのかはわっていないが、水稲とともに稲作農耕文化が大陸から伝わってきた弥生時代には、米を使った酒造りが行われたと考えられている。

　その後、奈良時代後半になると稲作も安定し、「造酒司（みきのつかさ）」という役所が設けられ、朝廷のための酒造りが行われた。日本酒の原型が形作られたのは室町時代で、原料の精米や、雑菌を繁殖させないように、酒を熱殺菌させる技術が確立した。

　さらに江戸時代には、香味を整え、酸敗を防ぐ方法として焼酎を加える技術も使われ、お酒を3回に分けて仕込む3段仕込みも完成させた。これが現在の酒造りの基となっているのだ。

When sake started to be made hasn't been clarified, but it is considered that sake has been made with rice since the Yayoi period when rice growing was introduced from China with paddy rice. In the late Nara period, rice growing had established and the sake brewing office called 'Miki-no-Tsukasa' was located in order to brew sake for the Imperial Court. It is the Muromachi period when a prototype of sake was built. The method of polishing rice and the heat sterilization technique to prevent propagation of various bacteria were established. In the Edo period, the technique of adding shochu as to control its flavor and not to be soured was used and Sandan-jikomi, the way of fermenting sake with three steps, was brought to completion. This is the foundation of current sake brewing.

The reputation of SAKE in overseas

日本酒の海外の評価

　2013年に和食がユネスコ文化遺産に登録され、和食とともに提供される日本酒にも、世界の注目が高まってきた。
　高級食材である和食には、質の高い日本酒が出されるので、初めて日本酒を口にした外国人は、原料が米とは思えない、果実の香りやきれいな味わいに驚くのだ。ロンドンで開催されるIWC（インターナショナル・ワイン・チャレンジ）SAKE部門、全米日本酒歓評会、フランスで催される日本酒コンテストKura Masterなどは、外国人の審査員が日本酒を評価する大会だ。本書では、外国人の審査員の舌をも魅了して栄冠に輝いた日本酒を中心に掲載した。ぜひ味わってほしい。

'Washoku' added to the UNESCO Heritage list in 2013 and sake provided with it is gathering more attention from all over the world. As high-class washoku is provided with high-quality sake, foreigners will be outtalked for its fruity aroma and pretty taste and won't believe that is made from rice when they taste it for the first time. There are some sake competitions where foreign jurors value sake such as IWC (International Wine Challenge) sake competition in London, U.S. National Sake Appraisal, Kura Master in France. This book mainly introduces to you sakes which fascinated them and won glorious awards. Let's try to taste them!

TYPES OF SAKE AND THE BREWING

日本酒の種類と作り方

Types of sake

Sake is basically classified by two points of view. The first point is what kinds of materials are used. Sake made only from rice and koji can be written Junmai-shu, but one that contains any other material cannot be do that. The second is how much part of rice is polished. The rate of polished rice is referred to as Seimai-buai (rice-polishing ratio). It is the percentage of rice that remains after milling to the original size. Depending on it sake is called by different names. That of Daiginjo-shu is less than 50%, that of Ginjo-shu is less than 60% and that of Honjozo-shu is less than 70%.

主な分類

日本酒の分類の基本は大きく分けて二つ。一つが原料。原料が米と米麹だけのものは、「純米酒」と表記できる。別の原料が混じった場合には表記できない。二つ目が米を削る量。玄米に対する削ったあとに残る米の量を「精米歩合」と呼び、精米歩合の違いで表記が異なる。大吟醸酒は精米歩合50%以下、吟醸酒は60%以下、本醸造酒は70%以下となる。

Junmai Daiginjo-shu
純米大吟醸酒

分類
Classification

精米分合
Rice-polishing rate

米
Rice

米麹
Koji

Rice-polishing rate : ～50%
精米歩合 50%以下

「獺祭　純米大吟醸　磨き二割三分」➡P.36
DASSAI MIGAKI NIWARISANBU

Made by milling luxuriously
more than half of
highest grade sake rice

**最高級の酒米を
半分以上贅沢に削って造る**

精米歩合が50%以下の米と米麹だけで造る、各蔵の最高ランクに位置する日本酒。米は外側ほど脂質やタンパク質など、酒の香味を落とす成分が多いので、削るほどきれいな味わいの酒に仕上がる。吟醸香と呼ばれる果実のような香りも特徴だ。

This is the finest sake which is made only from the rice, the rice-polishing rate of which is less than 50%, and koji. In the outside of rice, there are more components that degrade sake flavor such as fats and protein, so the more rice is milled, the clearer its taste becomes. The fruity aroma called 'Ginjo fragrance' is characteristic of this.

Junmai Ginjo-shu
純米吟醸酒

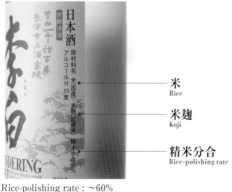

米
Rice

米麹
Koji

精米分合
Rice-polishing rate

Rice-polishing rate : ～60%
精米歩合 60%以下

「李白　純米吟醸　WANDERING POET」➡P.40
RIHAKU JUNMAIGINJO WANDERING POET

Completed to rich and
delicate sake
with taking much time
and effort

**手間暇掛けた吟醸造りで
芳醇で繊細な酒に仕上げる**

精米歩合が60%以下の米と米麹だけを使用し、大吟醸造りと同じように、酒のもとになる醪を低温でゆっくりと発酵させて醸す。糖分をアルコールと二酸化炭素に変える酵母の種類により、メロンやリンゴ、バラなど様々な果実香、花香が生まれる。

This sake is made only from the rice, the rice-polishing rate of which is less than 60%, and koji. It is made by fermenting and brewing the mash which is a material of sake slowly at low temperature. Depending on types of yeast that changes saccharide to alcohol and carbon dioxide, there are various flavors and aroma — various fruity and floral aromas.

Junmai-shu
純米酒

米
Rice

米麹
Koji

Rice-polishing rate : ──
精米歩合 （──）

「西の関　手造り純米酒」➡P.60
NISHINOSEKI TEZUKURIJYUNMAISHU

It has rich flavor of rice and is mostly drank with Washoku

米の味わい豊かで
和食に合う食中酒が多い

白米の米と米麹だけで造られた、香味や
色などが良好な酒。米の甘みや旨み、味
わいに膨らみを持つものが多い。日本酒
は冷酒から燗酒まで広い温度帯で楽しめ
るのが特徴だが、純米酒は燗にすると旨
みや味わいがさらに増すタイプが多い。

This sake has a good taste and color, made
only with polished rice and koji.Many of them
express sweeties and deliciousness of rice
that gives fullness.The characteristic of it is
that it can be enjoyed at a wide temperature
range, from cold to warm. Junmai-shu is especially tasty when it is warmed, increasing
in flavor and gaining an umami taste.

Daiginjo-shu
大吟醸酒

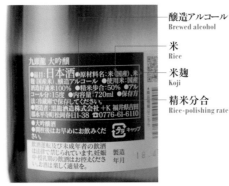

醸造アルコール
Brewed alcohol

米
Rice

米麹
Koji

精米分合
Rice-polishing rate

Rice-polishing rate : ～50%
精米歩合 50%以下

「九頭龍　大吟醸」➡P.64
KUZURYU DAIGINJO

Let's drink from wine glass and enjoy its ginjo fragrance

ワイングラスなどで
吟醸香を楽しもう

精米歩合が50％以下の米と米麹、基準値
以下の醸造アルコールだけで造られた、
純米大吟醸酒と双璧を成す最高級酒。醸
造アルコールを使う理由は、香りや味わい
をより際立たせて、後口の切れを引き出す
効果がある。お酒だけで楽しむのも一興。

This is the highest class sake that is equal to
Junmai Daiginjo. It is made only from the
rice, the rice-polishing rate of which is less
than 50%, koji and brewers alcohol which is
less than the reference value. The reason
why distilled alcohol is used is to emphasize
its flavor and taste and derive its sharpness
of aftertaste.

Ginjo-shu
吟醸酒

米
Rice

精米分合
Rice-polishing rate

醸造アルコール
Brewed alcohol

Rice-polishing rate : ～60%
精米歩合 60％以下
「吟醸 磯自慢」➡P.66
GINJO ISOJIMAN

Many of them match with French and Italian

フレンチやイタリアンとも
相性が良いタイプが多い

精米歩合が60％以下の米と米麹、基準値以下の醸造アルコールだけを原料に、低温発酵の吟醸造りで醸され、果実のような香りも。大吟醸酒や吟醸酒は温度変化にデリケートで、貯蔵も低温で管理され、冷たいまま味わうのがおすすめ。

This sake is made only from the rice, the rice-polishing rate of which is less than 60%, koji and brewers alcohol which is less than the reference value. It is brewed by fermenting at low temperature (Ginjo-zukuri), and has fruity aroma. Daiginjo-shu and Ginjo-shu are recommended to taste them as they are cold.

Honjozo-shu
本醸造酒

精米分合
Rice-polishing rate

醸造アルコール
Brewed alcohol

米
Rice

米麹
Koji

Rice-polishing rate : ～70%
精米歩合 70％以下
「月の桂 大極上中汲にごり酒 本醸造」➡P.76
TSUKINOKATSURA

It is good for biginners because of its smooth and mild taste

淡麗でまろやか
初心者にも飲みやすい

精米歩合が70％以下の米と米麹、基準値以下の醸造アルコールだけで造られ、香味や色などが良好な酒。冷酒、燗酒どちらでも楽しめるタイプが多く、醸造アルコールの効果で、後味に切れの良さが加わるのも特徴。食中酒としても最適だ。

This sake is made only from the rice, the rice-polishing rate of which is less than 70%, koji and brewers alcohol which is less than the reference value. It has good tastes and color. Most of it can be tasted both as cold and hot sake. The characteristic of it is a refreshing aftertaste in effect of brewers alcohole. It is best to enjoy with a meal.

Futsu-shu(Non-preminm)
普通酒

Rice — 米

Koji — 米麹

Rice-polishing rate : ──
精米歩合（──）

「蓬莱　天才杜氏の入魂酒」➡P.74
HOURAI TEMSAITOJINO NYUKONSHU

The standard sake of sake breweries aiming at cheep and good

安い！旨い！を目指す
酒蔵の定番酒

精米歩合に定めはなく、白米の米、米麹を原料に、醸造アルコール及び定められた糖類や酸味料などを副原料にして造られる、晩酌用の酒。地方の酒蔵では、地元の要望で造るケースも多く、蔵の実力が試される酒だ。普通酒の表記はない。

This is evening drinking sake, made from polished rice and koji as principal materials and brewers alcohol and prescribed saccharides and acidifiers as sub-materials. Its rice polishing rate is not specified. Many local sake breweries have been brewing it at local customers' request. 'Futsu-shu' is not shown on commodity labels.

Koshu(Aged sake)
古酒

Classification — 分類

Rice — 米

Koji — 米麹

Rice-polishing rate : ──
精米歩合（──）

「華鳩　貴醸酒　8年貯蔵」➡P.75
HANAHATO KIJOSHU 8NENCHOZO

Very popular with foreigners for its the golden brown and sweetness

琥珀色の深い味わいは
外国でも人気が高い

日本酒は通常1年のサイクルで製造、消費されるが、一定の環境の中で貯蔵され、5年、10年を経て出荷されるものもある。3年以上の熟成酒を「長期熟成酒」と呼ぶこともある。甘く濃厚な味わいはまさに、シェリー酒やポートワインを彷彿させる。

Generally, Japanese sake is brewed and shipped in a year cycle, but some are stored in a certain environment for 5-10 years and shipped. Sake aged more than 3 years is sometimes called "long-term aging sake". Its sweet and rich taste has a strong resemblance to sherry wine or port.

Sparkling sake
スパークリング日本酒

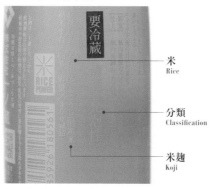

米
Rice

分類
Classification

米麹
Koji

Rice-polishing rate : ——
精米歩合 （——）
「一ノ蔵 発泡清酒 すず音」➡P.77
ICHINOKURA SPARKLING SAKE SUZUNE

Popular to women and the best drink for toast

女性にも大人気！
乾杯酒としても最適だ

炭酸ガスを含んだ日本酒のこと。製法は、シャンパーニュと同じ方法の瓶内2次発酵方式、発酵している最中の酒を濾過せず菌が生きている状態で瓶詰めする方式、炭酸ガス注入方式がある。アルコール分も低めから高いものまであり、種類も豊富。

This is a sake containing carbonic acid gas. There are three manufacturing methods — The first is an in-bottle secondary fermentation method which is same as that of champagne. The second is a non-filtering method to bottle fermenting sake with keeping yeast active. The third is a carbonic acid gas injection method. There are various kins of sparkling sake, from weak to strong.

Kioke Shikomi(Wooden-bucket prepared sake)
木桶仕込の酒

分類
Classification

Rice-polishing rate : ——
精米歩合 （——）
「澤乃井 木桶仕込 彩は」➡P.78
SAWANOI KIOKEJIKOMI IROHA

Sake filled with a tradition and techniques of Japanese sake brewing

日本の酒造りの
伝統と技が詰まった酒

明治時代まで、酒は杉の大桶で造られていた。こうした酒造りを復活させようと造られたのが、木桶仕込の酒だ。製法も自然界の乳酸菌を利用する、昔からの生酛（きもと）造りや山廃（やまはい）造りが用いられることが多い。

Sake had been made using a big cedar barrel until the Meiji period. Brewing Kioke-jikomi sake was started with the attempt to restore this traditional sake brewing. Most of its manufacturing method adopt ancient brewing method such as Kimotozukuri or Yamahaizukuri.

Specialized names derived from the manufacturing method and so on

製法などに由来する特徴的な呼称

日本酒のラベルには、造り方や搾り方、火入れ（加熱処理）や貯蔵の仕方など、酒についての様々な特徴も書かれてある。その特徴を知ると、日本酒がさらに楽しめる。

On the label of sake, various characteristics are printed — how to brew, press, heat, stock and so on. It is sure that you can be more delightful to taste sake after knowing them.

Kimotozukuri

生酛造り

日本酒では、まず酒のもと（酛）を造り酵母を純粋培養する。その際に、自然界の乳酸菌を利用する、昔から伝わる製法。力強い酒質が特徴だ。

The first process of brewing sake is a pure culture of yeast to sake seed mash. Kimotozukuri is a traditional method of using lactic acid bacteria in this step. Sake made by this method is characteristics of strong taste.

Yamahai-shikomi

山廃仕込み

生酛造りで、米と米麹をすり潰す作業を「山卸」と呼ぶ。明治時代、酵素の作用で同じ効果が出ることがわかり、山卸を廃止したため「山廃」。

In the Kimotozukuri method, the process of mixing rice and koji into a puree is called Yamaorosi. In the Meiji period, it turned out that it can also be done by function of enzyme and Yamaorosi process was abolished. This new method was called Yamahai.

Nigorizake

にごり酒

目の粗い布などで濾しただけの、白く濁っている酒。加熱殺菌していないものは、活性にごり酒という。

This sake is cloudy sake just made by filtering with a coarse cloth. One which is not pasteurized is called Kassei-nigorizake.

Muroka-Namagenshu

無濾過生酒原酒

濾過や火入れをしていないので、豊かな風味が楽しめる。加水もしないので、アルコール度数も強い。

As these sake are not filtered and heated, you can enjoy their rich flavor. They have high alcohol content because not added water.

[freshly pressed sake]
Shiboritate

しぼりたて

蔵で搾ってすぐ出荷される酒。でき立ての酒なのでフレッシュな味わいが楽しめる。

Sake shipped immediately after pressing in a sake brewery. It has a fresh taste.

Fukuro-sibori

袋搾り

大吟醸など高級酒に用いられる搾りの方法。醪を酒袋に入れて吊るし、圧力をかけずに滴らせる。

The press method for premium sake like Daiginjo. To put the fermentation mash into a sake bag and drip with no pressure.

Namachozo-shu/
Namazume-shu
生貯蔵酒・生詰酒

生貯蔵酒は、生で貯蔵して瓶詰め時に1回火入れ。生詰酒は1回火入れしたあと貯蔵し、生で瓶詰め。

Namachozo-shu is stored raw and pasteurized once when bottling. Namazume-shu is stored after pasteurized once and then bottled raw.

Hiyaoroshi

冷やおろし

春先にでき上がった新酒は、ひと夏寝かすと荒々しさが取れほど良く熟す。秋口に出荷される生詰酒だ。

New sake completed in early spring becomes aged well and the wildness of its taste is removed after stored during the summer. It is shipmented in the autumn.

Process of brewing sake

Sake is the brewage which is made by the most ingenious and complex method in the world. It is different from other brewages in the parallel complex fermentation. First step is to produce koji and convert the starch of steamed rice into sugar by its diastatic enzyme. The yeast converts this sugar into carbon dioxide and alcohol. This simultaneous process of two steps is unique in sake brewing.

日本酒ができるまで

日本酒は世界で最も巧妙で複雑な造りをする醸造酒だ。ほかの醸造酒との大きな違いは、「並行複発酵」という仕込み方にある。まず麹を造り、麹が持つ糖化酵素によって、蒸上がった米のデンプンを糖に変える。この糖を培養された酵母が食べ、二酸化炭素とアルコールに変える。日本酒造りでは、この二つの工程が並行して同時に行われるのが特徴だ。

1

Rice-polishing →Rice-washing → Rice-soaking
精米→洗米→浸漬

酒造りはまず精米から始まる。通常の飯米は精米歩合90%くらいだが、酒に使用する米は最高ランクの大吟醸だと、2昼夜以上かけて50%以下にまで削る。次に付着した糠などを専用の洗米機で洗い落としたあと、米を水に一定時間浸けて水分を吸わせる。

Sake brewing starts by polishing rice. Rice-polishing rate of cooked rice is generally about 90%, but rice for premium Daiginjo is polished for over two days until that of it reaches 50%. In the next step, the rice is washed off remaining dirt like rice bran powder in a rice washer and soaked into water for a definite period of time.

2

Rice-steaming → cooling
蒸米→放冷

水を吸わせる際、精米歩合が低いほど吸水時間が早くなるので、杜氏も秒単位で指示する。吸水後は蒸気で蒸したあと、放冷機などで冷ます。蒸米にする理由は、麹が持つ糖化酵素の作用を受けやすくするためと、外硬内軟になった米は麹造りにも適するからだ。

The less rice-polishing rate is, the faster rice absorbs water so when soaking rice into water, a chief sake maker gives directions in seconds. Then, it is steamed and cooled in a rice cooler. The reason why rice is steamed is to make more susceptible to the action of the koji diastatic enzyme and more suitable for koji-making with the outside dried out and the inside soft.

3

[Malt-growing]
Koji-tsukuri
製麹（麹造り）

日本酒造りの中で「一麹、二酛、三造り（醪）」といわれる重要な作業だ。まず、温度約28度、湿度約70％の蒸し暑い麹室（むろ）と呼ばれる作業場に蒸米を広げる。そして種麹を振りかけてよく混ぜて布をかぶせ、時間ごとに攪拌（かくはん）して麹菌を増殖させる。約2日間で完成だ。

This is an essential step of sake brewing as it is said "First, koji. Second, moto, and third tsukuri." At first, to spread steamed rice on the table called 'Koji-muro', where it is hot and humid kept in an environment at about 28℃ at about 70% humidity. Next, to powder it with spores of koji mold, mix well, cover with a cloth and agitate them every fixed time period to promote the growth of koji mold. It takes about two days.

4

Sake mash-making
酒母造り（酛造り）

酒母は、蒸米、水、麹に酵母を加え、醪の発酵に大切な役割を果たす酵母を大量に培養したもので、雑菌の増殖を抑える乳酸も含まれる。この乳酸菌を自然界から得るのが生酛系酒母（山廃酛も含む）、醸造用乳酸を添加したものは速醸系酒母（ラベルには表示なし）という。

The yeast takes an important part of moromi fermenting. A yeast mash is cultivated yeast by adding yeast to steamed rice, water and koij. It contains lactic acid which suppresses the proliferation of undesirable microbes. The method of using this natural bacteria is called Kimoto-style starter culture (including Yamaha-style) and that of adding lactic acid bacteria for brewing is called Sokujo-kei (unprinted on label).

5 Preparation for fermentation mash

(Three step preparation:First addition, Second addition, Final addition) → fermentation mash

仕込み（3段仕込み　初添え、仲添え、留添え）→ 発酵（もろみ）

日本酒は3回に分けて仕込まれる。初日は「初添え」で、酒母に麹と水を加え、その後蒸米を入れる。2日目は「踊り」で、酵母の増殖を図るための休日だ。3日目「仲添え」、4日目「留添え」では、麹と蒸米、水を増やしながら投入する。こうして造られたものが醪で、発酵しながら酒となる。

Sake is fermented in three steps. First step takes two days. On the first day, to add koji and water to a yeast starter and then add steamed rice(first fermentation). The second day is the resting stage called Odori to promote the growth of the yeast. In the second addition on day 3 and final addition on day 4, to add koji, steamed rice and water little by little. Moromi, fermentation mash, is made in such way and it becomes sake after fermenting

6 Pressing → Racking/Filtering/Pesteurizing

上槽（搾り）→ おり引き・濾過・火入れ

醪は約20日間かけて酒になるが、吟醸造りでは30日以上もかかる。醪は圧搾機で搾り酒と酒かすに分ける。酒をタンクに貯蔵したあと、不純物を沈殿させて上澄みを抜き（おり引き）、濾過器で雑味成分や色を取り、加熱殺菌（火入れ）する。

The fermentation mash is usually fermented to sake for about 20 days, but it takes over 30 days in Ginjo-zukuri. The mash is divided to pressed sake and sake kasu by a filter press. The pressed sake is stored in a sake tank until the impurities are sedimented. And then, to draw a transparent upper layer (Racking), to get rid of components exhibiting foreign flavor and colored through a filter (Filtering) and to heat sterilize (Pasteurizing).

7

Tank-storing →Water-adding → Pasteurizing →Bottling
タンク貯蔵→割水→火入れ→瓶詰

加熱殺菌された酒は貯蔵タンクに送られる。原酒はアルコール度数が20度を超えるものもあるので、水を加え（割水）、酒質に合わせて調整する。15度〜16度が一般的。出荷する前に2度目の火入れをして酒を65度まで加熱。瓶詰めしたあと急速に冷却して完成だ。

Pasteurized sake is transferred to storage tanks. The alcohol content of some brewers sake is over 20% so it is generally adjusted for quality of sake by adding water to 15-16%. It is secondly heated to 65℃ before a shipment. And then, it is bottled and chilled immediately to perfection.

協力／小澤酒造
Cooperation / Ozawa Shuzo

| Column |

Sake and shrine ritual
日本酒と神事

瑞穂の国・日本には酒の神様を祀る神社が多い。なかでも、大神神社（奈良）、松尾大社（京都）、梅宮大社（京都）は、日本三大酒神神社として有名だ。酒蔵には酒の神様を祀る神社の神棚があり、造り初めには蔵人総出で酒造りの無事を祈願する。

There are many shrines to the god of sake in the Land of Rice-plants, Japan. Among them, Omiwa-Jinja Shrine in Nara, Matsuo-Taisha Shrine and Umemiya-Taisya Shrine in Kyoto are famous as the top 3 sake shrine in Japan. Sake breweries have Kamidana (household Shinto altar) and all the brewer pray for the safe of brewing at the beginning. of brewing season.

ALL ABOUT SAKE

日本酒大全

Map of Sake

全国の酒マップ

Junmai Daiginjo-shu, Junmai Ginjo-shu

純米大吟醸酒・純米吟醸酒

　各蔵が名誉をかけて造る最高峰の日本酒は、吟醸造りで醸された果実のような香りと米に由来する甘い旨みが特徴だ。その味わいの豊かさは、世界の人々の舌を驚かせ、日本酒への興味を膨らませ続けている。ここでは、その原動力ともなった輝きに満ちた日本酒を紹介する。

The highest-class Japanese sake made on the brewery's honor has fruity aroma and sweet flavor comes from rice. The richness of taste amazes tongues of people around the world and grows the interest toward Japanese sake. This section introduces glorious Japanese sake which motivates the interest.

DEWAZAKURA ICHIRO

Junmai Daiginjo / 出羽桜　純米大吟醸　一路

Yamagata / 山形

Clearness of snowy region
雪国ならではの透明感

「フルーティーな香りと、ふくよかな味わい」の吟醸造りを追求し続ける出羽桜酒造の純米大吟醸。雪解け水のような透明感を持ちながら、純米大吟醸ならではの米の上品な甘みと旨みが、口中にまろやかに広がる。

A top-quality product manufactured by Dewazakura Sake Brewery Co.,Ltd. which keeps on seeking "Fruity aroma and subtle, full taste" ginjo making. It has clearness like snowmelt and a unique, refined sweetness and flavor of Junmai Daiginjo rice is mellowly filled in your mouth.

甘辛度
Sweet-dryness

甘 ——————— 辛
Sweet　　　　　Dry

味わい
Taste

淡麗 ——————— 濃醇
Light　　　　　Rich

香り
Aroma

低 ——————— 高
Weak　　　　　Strong

原料米 山田錦
酵母 小川酵母　アルコール度数 15　日本酒度 +4
酸度 1.3　精米分合 45%　小売価格 2800円 720ml
Raw material rice: Yamada Nishiki
Yeast: Ogawa Kobo　Alcohol content: 15%
Sake meter value: +4　Acidity: 1.3
Rice-polishing rate: 45%　Retail price: 2800yen/720ml

Ginjo-making of long-term low temperature fermentation
長期低温発酵の吟醸造り

軟水の奥羽山系の伏流水を仕込み水にしているので、やさしい味わいを醸し出す。酒造りの特徴は、長期間低温発酵での醪（もろみ）の仕込み。米の旨味が最大限に引き出され、厳しい環境におかれた酵母からは酵母の涙といわれる果実のような吟醸香が分泌される。お酒は少し冷やし、山菜の天ぷらなどとの組み合わせがおすすめだ。

Since soft, river-bed water from Ou mountains is used for the sake-making, it creates the mild taste. Moromi (sake mash) is fermented at low temperature for many hours. From the process, full flavor of rice is extracted. Fruity ginjo-aroma which is called tears from yeast comes out of yeast made under a tough environment. It is recommended to chill the sake a little and enjoy with tempura of mountain vegetables.

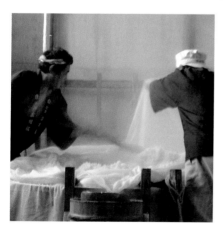

Ginjo brewery well-known nationwide
全国に名を馳せる吟醸蔵

蔵の創業は明治25年（1892）。昭和55年（1980）に発売した吟醸酒が旨いと大評判に。それが吟醸酒ブームの発端となり、吟醸蔵として全国に名を馳せた。IWCのSAKE部門では「出羽桜　一路」が最高賞の「チャンピオン・サケ」を獲得。世界の人からの注目度も高い。天童市は名湯の町としても知られる。

The brewery was founded in Meiji 25 (1892). Ginjo-shu released in Showa 55 (1980) became highly popular with its taste. It triggered Ginjo-shu boom and the brewery became known nationwide. "Dewazakura Ichiro" won "Champion Sake" which is the top honor of Sake division of IWC (International Wine Challenge). It draws attention around the world. Tendo-city is also known with Onsen.

DEWAZAKURA SAKE BREWERY　出羽桜酒造

🏠 〒994-0044　山形県天童市一日町一丁目4番6号　☎ 023-653-5121　**酒蔵見学** 不可（蔵敷地内にある古い陶磁器の酒器や工芸品などを展示公開する「出羽桜美術館」は見学可能）　**URL** http://www.dewazakura.co.jp/
Add: 1-4-6, Hitoichimachi, Tendo-City, Yamagata-Pref., 994-0044　**Tel:** +81 23-653-5121　**Brewery tour:** NO (You can visit "Dewazakura Art Museum" in the brewery property which exhibits old ceramics, porcelains and handicrafts.)　**URL:** http://www.dewazakura.co.jp/

KOSHINOKANBAI KINMUKU

Junmai Daiginjo ／ 純米大吟醸　越乃寒梅　金無垢

Niigata ／ 新潟

Reigning as an unshaken popular brand

不動の人気銘柄として君臨

昭和から人気の越乃寒梅は、さわりなく飲める淡麗タイプで、米本来の旨さを感じられる酒質。金無垢は長期低温発酵と低温熟成で、上品な吟醸香と香味を表現している。どの温度帯でも楽しめるが、ぬる燗が旨い。

Koshinokanbai which has been popular since Showa era is a subtle type which is palatable, and you can feel the taste of rice. Kinmuku expresses refined Ginjo aroma and flavor by a long-term low temperature fermentation and low temperature aging. It is enjoyable in any temperature, but Nurukan (lukewarm) is recommended.

034

甘辛度
Sweet-dryness

甘　　　　　辛
Sweet　　　Dry

味わい
Taste

淡麗　　　　濃醇
Light　　　Rich

香り
Aroma

低　　　　　高
Weak　　　Strong

原料米　山田錦
酵母　非公開　　アルコール度数　16　　日本酒度　+3
酸度　非公開　　精米歩合　35%　　小売価格　4300円　720ml
Raw material rice: Yamada Nishiki
Yeast: Closed　　Alcohol content: 16%
Sake meter value: +3　　Acidity: Closed
Rice-polishing rate: 35%　　Retail price: 4300yen/720ml

（成分値は管理目標）

Applying traditional craftmanship
伝統的な職人技を駆使

新潟県は90を超える酒蔵がある酒処。蔵のある亀田郷も、阿賀野川や信濃川に囲まれた水豊かな砂丘地で、川の伏流水を仕込み水とする酒造りの好適地だ。金無垢は最高品質の山田錦を35%までていねいに磨き、麹造りから発酵、熟成まで、長年培ってきた確かな技術と蔵人のチームワークを駆使して醸される。

This one of 90 breweries in Niigata prefecture is at Kamedagou, a duneland abundant in water surrounded by rivers of Agano and Shinano, and suitable for sake-making to use river-bed water. Kinmuku, using the top-quality Yamada Nishiki polished to 35%, is made with traditional techniques like aging control with low temperature, a box koji method and Fune pressing. It matches well with raw Iwagaki oysters which have salty and strong flavor.

Compassion to locals
地元への思いが詰まる

蔵の創業は明治40年(1907)。「地元の人に旨い酒を提供したい」その創業時の思いは、戦後の米不足の時も変わらず、少量でも高精白でいい酒をという理念を貫き通して今に至る。約14万人が訪れる地元開催の「にいがた酒の陣」にも毎年出展しており、味わいながら蔵元と交流ができる貴重な機会となっている。

The brewery was founded in Meiji 40 (1907). "To serve tasty sake for local people," the philosophy has been kept since its foundation to serve good sake with highly polished rice even a little during a shortage of rice after the war. Hoping people enjoy their sake well even with a small amount, they ship the products with 16% of alcohol content which is 1% higher. "Niigata Sakenojin" event about 120,000 people visit, is held locally.

ISHIMOTO SAKE BREWERY　石本酒造

〒950-0116　新潟県新潟市江南区北山847-1　025-276-2028 (8時～17時)　酒蔵見学 不可　URL http://koshinokanbai.co.jp/
Add: 847-1 Kitayama, Konan-ku, Niigata-shi, Niigata Prefecture 950-0116　Tel: +81-25-276-2028 (8am-5pm)　Brewery tour: NO　URL: http://koshinokanbai.com/

DASSAI MIGAKI NIWARISANBU

Junmai Daiginjo ／ 獺祭　純米大吟醸　磨き二割三分

yamaguchi ／山口

Surprisingly 23% of rice-polishing rate!

精米歩合23%の衝撃!

洋梨のような爽涼な香り、ピュアなハチミツのような甘み、飲んだあとは雑味を残さない切れの良さ。この絶妙なバランスとともに香味の余韻も長く続く。日本人の舌を高級白ワインから日本酒へと回帰させた逸品だ。

Pear-like refreshing aroma, sweetness like pure honey and sharp aftertaste without off-flavor. With the fine balance, the aroma and taste remain long. This excellent sake made Japanese tongues to go back to Japanese sake from high-class white wines.

原料米 山田錦
酵母 非公開　アルコール度数 16　日本酒度 非公開
酸度 非公開　精米歩合 23%　小売価格 4762円　720ml
Raw material rice: Yamada Nishiki
Yeast: Closed　Alcohol content: 16%
Sake meter value: Closed　Acidity: Closed
Rice-polishing rate: 23%　Retail price: 4762yen/720ml

甘辛度
Sweet-dryness

甘　　　　　辛
Sweet　　　　Dry

味わい
Taste

淡麗　　　　濃醇
Light　　　　Rich

香り
Aroma

低　　　　　高
Weak　　　　Strong

Sake-making for the future
未来を見つめた酒造り

日本酒は米を削るほど味わいが透き通り、きれいな酒になるといわれている。伝統の技と最新式の機械を融合し、未来に向けた酒造りに挑む獺祭は、米を50％以上削った最高峰の純米大吟醸しか造らないが、磨き二割三分はさらに77％まで米を削って醸す究極の純米大吟醸だ。

It is said that the taste of Japanese sake becomes more clear and beautiful as rice is polished more. Combining traditional techniques and state of the art machines, Dassai is made challenging sake-making for the future. Dassai is only made top-class Daiginjo with rice 50% of the grain has been polished away. Migaki Niwarisanbu is an ultimate Junmai Ginjo-shu made with rice 77% of the grain has been polished away.

Deep in the mountains pursuing ideal sake
理想の水を求めて山奥に

蔵の創業は昭和23年(1947)。蔵の側を流れる島田川の伏流水が仕込み水で、ミネラル豊富なまろやかな水質が獺祭の舌ざわりの良さの原点だ。獺祭の名は、獺に纏わる現地名にちなむ。岩国市の山奥に近年完成した巨大な白亜の本社蔵はまさに驚きだが、内部の白で統一された獺祭ストアで飲む酒の旨さは絶品で訪れる価値がある。

The brewery was founded in Showa 23 (1947). River-bed water from Shimata river running by the brewery is used. Mineral-rich and mild water quality is the origin of Dassai which has fine texture. Dassai is named after a local site related to otters. Recently, the brewery built a large, white-chalk head-quarter building deep in the mountains of Iwakuni-shi which might surprise you.

ASAHI SHUZO　旭酒造

〒742-0422　山口県岩国市周東町獺越2167-4　☎ 0827-86-0120　**酒蔵見学** 可(要予約、1日2回　1回約40分　1回目11時〜、2回目14時〜)　**URL** https://www.asahishuzo.ne.jp/

Add: 2167-4, Osogoe, Shutomachi, Iwakuni-shi, Yamaguchi, 742-0422,　**Tel:** +81-827-86-0120　**Brewery tour:** YES (first Brewery tour: 11am, second tour 2pm. About 40 mins)　**URL:** https://www.asahishuzo.ne.jp/

HITAKAMI YASUKE

Junmai Ginjo-shu / 日高見　純米吟醸　弥助

Miyagi / 宮城

Supreme mariage with Sushi

寿司=至高のマリアージュ

寿司に惚れこんだが蔵元が、日本一寿司に合う酒を造ろうと歳月をかけて完成させた純米吟醸酒。寿司と一緒に口に含むと、魚介の旨み甘みに寄り添い、まろやかに包み込んだあと、切れの良さが口を洗う芸術品だ。

The brewery owner who loves Sushi tried to produce sake matched with sushi the best in Japan and took time and effort to produce this Junmai Ginjo-shu. When you sip it with Sushi, it matches with savory and sweetness of fishes tenderly. This sake is an artifact to wrap the savory mellowly and sharp after-taste which washes your mouth.

甘辛度
Sweet-dryness

甘　　　　　辛
Sweet　　　　Dry

味わい
Taste

淡麗　　　　濃醇
Light　　　　Rich

香り
Aroma

低　　　　　高
Weak　　　　Strong

原料米 蔵の華
酵母 宮城酵母　アルコール度数 16　日本酒度 +7
酸度 1.5　精米分合 50%　小売価格 1800円 720ml
Raw material rice: Kura no Hana
Yeast: Miyagi Kobo　Alcohol content: 16%
Sake meter value: +7　Acidity: 1.5
Rice-polishing rate: 50%　Retail price: 1800yen/720ml

Clean dry sake produced by a fishing port
漁港が育んだきれいな辛口酒

目の前は「世界三大漁場」のひとつに数えられる三陸沖で、毎日新鮮な魚介が水揚げされる。最新式の洗米機や放冷機も導入し、徹底した温度管理で気品ある伸びやかな辛口に仕上げた酒は、港町ならではの酒として高級料亭でも引っ張りだこだ。冷やでもぬる燗でも旨い。

Ocean fresh seafoods are landed every day from Sanrikuoki, one of "the world's three largest fishing grounds" in front of the brewery. Installing state of the art rice washing machine and cooling machine, with a careful temperature control, refined long-lasting and dry taste is made. This sake representing the port town is popular among high-class Japanese style restaurants and so on.

Yasuke's name related to Japanese culture
日本文化に纏わる酒名・弥助

蔵の創業は文久元年 (1861)。「弥助」とは歌舞伎などの演目「義経千本桜」で、源平合戦に敗れた敗軍の将が寿司屋に逃げ込んだ際に使った偽名だ。この話から明治から昭和にかけての花柳界では、寿司のことを弥助と呼ぶようになったのが語源という。石巻には地物の新鮮な魚介を扱う寿司屋が数多く、寿司屋巡りも楽しめる。

The brewery was founded in Bunkyu 1 (1861). "Yasuke" is a false name used by a general who lost at Genpei war and run off into Sushi shop in Kabuki play called "Yoshitsune Senbon Zakura". From the play, sushi was called Yasuke from Meiji to Showa era among Geisha. There are lots of Sushi shops to serve local, fresh seafoods in Ishinomaki. Let's enjoy visiting the sushi shops with the history of Yasuke.

HIRAKO SHUZO　平孝酒造

🏠 〒986-0871　宮城県石巻市清水町1丁目5-3　☎ 0225-22-0161　**酒蔵見学** 不可
Add: 1-5-3 Shimizu-cho, Ishinomaki-shi, Miyagi 986-0871　**Tel:** +81-225-22-0161　**Brewery tour:** NO

RIHAKU JUNMAIGINJO WANDERING POET

Junmai Ginjo-shu ／ 李白　純米吟醸　WANDERING POET

Shimane ／ 島根

Sake for meals attracts foreign gourmets

外国人の食通も魅了する食中酒

昭和の後半からの地酒ブームを牽引した銘醸蔵として知られ、すべて酒造好適米のみを原料として酒を醸す。穏やかな花香、ほど良い旨みとコク、酸が押す切れのいい後口。幅広い温度帯で楽しめる、食通垂涎の食中酒。

Known as an eminent brewery leading local sake boom since late Showa era. Only suitable rice for sake-making is used as the ingredient. Mild floral aroma, modest flavor and richness, and sharp aftertaste with sourness. It tastes good in any temperature and stimulates your appetite during a meal.

原料米 山田錦
酵母 61 K-1　アルコール度数 15　日本酒度 +4
酸度 1.7　精米分合 55%　小売価格 1560円 720ml
Raw material rice: Yamada Nishiki
Yeast: 61 K-1　Alcohol content: 15%
Sake meter value: +4　Acidity: 1.7
Rice-polishing rate: 55%　Retail price: 1560yen/720ml

甘辛度
Sweet-dryness

甘　　　　　辛
Sweet　　　　Dry

味わい
Taste

淡麗　　　　濃醇
Light　　　　Rich

香り
Aroma

低　　　　　高
Weak　　　　Strong

High-quality local sake exported overseas
質の高い地酒で海外進出

蔵では日本酒の普及を兼ね、1980年代よりいち早く海外輸出を積極的に展開した。中でも「WANDERRING POET」（放浪詩人）の名は、「李白」をイメージしやすいと諸外国での評判が高く、優れた高級酒として海外の食通達をも楽しませている。日本では気取らず、地元の名産あご（飛魚）野焼きやおでんとともに楽しんでみよう。

The brewery actively exports their productsfrom 1980s. Especially, this "Wandering Poet"is popular abroad by its name to evoke an image of"Li Bai". This high-class sake pleases foreign gourmets. Let's enjoy it casually in Japan with a local specialtyGrilled Ago (flying fishes) or Oden (Fishcake stew).

Let's visit Izumotaisha
出雲大社にも参拝しよう

蔵の創業は明治15年（1882）。島根県は出雲神話に登場する酒造りの発祥地。蔵は水と緑豊かな松江市にあり、仕込み水に使われる自社の「石橋の大井戸」は島根三名水のひとつに数えられる。舌ざわりがなめらかな甘露な軟水を使い出雲杜氏が醸した酒を飲むと、ヤマタノオロチを虜にした神話が目の前によみがえるようだ。

The brewery was founded in Meiji 15 (1882). Sake-making originated in Shimane-prefecture and it was mentioned in Izumo myths. The brewery is at Matsue-shi abundant in water and green. Water for the sake-making is from their "Ishibashi no Oido" (A well of Ishibashi) which is one of the most famous three waters in Shimane. Drinking sake made by Izumo brew master using smooth, sweet and soft water makes you to trip into the myth Yamatanoorochi gets drunk.

RIHAKU Sake Brewing　李白酒造

(住) 〒690-0881 島根県松江市石橋町335番地　(電) 0852-26-5555 試飲コーナー専用ダイヤル 090-9733-8539（土日祝のみ）　酒蔵見学 酒蔵見学は不可だが、試飲コーナーがあり10種類ほどのお酒が用意されている。　URL http://www.rihaku.co.jp/
Add: 335 Ishibashi-cho, Matsue-shi, Shimane 690-0881　Tel: +81-852-26-5555　Brewery tour: NO, but tasting about 10 products is available.　URL: http://www.rihaku.co.jp/

SHICHIDA OMACHI50

Junmai Ginjo-shu / 七田　純米吟醸　雄町50

Saga / 佐賀

Flavor of Sake rice
Omachi sparkles

酒米・雄町の旨さが煌めく

青いメロンのような香り、優しい舌ざわり、雄町という酒米ならではの、密度ある豊かな米の甘い旨みとほど良い酸味。飲んだ後の切れも良く、すべてにバランスがとれた純米吟醸。ボトルも粋でハレの日にも最適だ。

Sweet aroma like a green melon, mild texture, dense, rich and sweet flavor of Omachi rice for sake and modest sourness. This Junmai Ginjo also has a sharp aftertaste and well-balanced in every way. The stylish bottle is perfect for celebrations.

甘辛度
Sweet-dryness

甘		辛
Sweet		Dry

味わい
Taste

淡麗		濃醇
Light		Rich

香り
Aroma

低		高
Weak		Strong

原料米 雄町
酵母 非公開　アルコール度数 16　日本酒度 +2.8
酸度 1.4　精米分合 50%　小売価格 1650円　720ml

Raw material rice: Omachi
Yeast: Closed　Alcohol content: 16%
Sake meter value: +2.8　Acidity: 1.4
Rice-polishing rate: 50%　Retail price: 1650 yen/720 ml

The brewery grows rice
酒米栽培にも取り組む

平成10年より、自社製造部を中心に山田錦の栽培と研究を開始。地元の農家とともに「天山酒米栽培研究会」を立ち上げ、山田錦栽培にも取り組んでいる。雄町は精米後の吸水や醪の発酵管理が非常に難しいが、難題をクリアすると驚くほどの豊饒な味わいの酒となる。

From Heisei 10 (1998), the brewery started to grow and study Yamada Nishiki mainly at their manufacturing division. With local farmers, the brewery founded "Tenzan rice for sake cultivation study group" and also grows Omachi rice. Omachi is difficult to absorb water after rice polishing and control fermentation of moromi, but the taste comes out surprisingly rich after passing all of hard work.

Genji fireflies dance in front of the brewery
蔵前では源氏ボタルが舞う

蔵の創業は明治8年（1875）。蔵前には、天山山系が源流で源氏ボタルの発祥地ともいわれる、祇園川が流れる。蔵の仕込み水も天山の湧き水。水質はミネラル分を豊富に含み日本には珍しい硬水で、しっかりした味わいの男酒になるのも特徴だ。雄町50は「Kura Master」で最優秀賞のプレジデント賞を受賞、世界からも大注目。

The brewery was founded in Meiji 8 (1875). Gion River which is originated from Tenzan mountains and called as a home of Genji fireflies runs in front of the brewery. Spring water from Tenzan mountains is used for Sake-making. The water is rich in minerals and hard which is rare in Japan makes the manly, firm taste. OMACHI50 won the president award which is the top honor of "Kura Master" award.

TENZAN Sake Brewer　天山酒造

〒845-0003　佐賀県小城市小城町岩蔵1520　☎ 0952-73-3141　酒蔵見学 可（事前予約）農業や酒造りができる体験イベント「人米酒プロジェクト」も実施中。詳しくはHPで。　URL http://www.tenzan.co.jp/main/

Add: 1520 Iwakura Ogi-machi Ogi-shi Saga, 845-0003　**Tel:** +81-952-73-3141　**Brewery tour:** YES (Reservation required) For the details of "Jinmaishu project" event you can experience farming and sake-making, visit the HP below. **URL:** http://www.tenzan.co.jp/en/main/

Special Junmai-shu, Junmai-shu

特別純米酒・純米酒

米は日本の文化そのものだ。米で醸す日本酒には、日本古来の伝統と技術も詰まっている。米と米麹だけを原料にして造る純米酒は、まさに一滴一滴が日本文化の貴重な雫だ。ここでは、そんな米への思いを込めて造られた日本酒を紹介する。

Rice is the Japanese culture itself. Japanese sake made with rice is filled with Japanese old traditions and technologies. Every drop of Junmai-shu made by only rice and rice koji is a precious dewdrop of Japanese culture. This section introduces Japanese sake made with the passion for rice.

DENSHU

Special Junmai-shu / 田酒　特別純米酒

Aomori ／ 青森

Gasp at the taste of Kan-agari!

燗上がりの旨さに絶句！

燗にしてますますうまくなることを「燗上がりする」といい、その変化が楽しめる酒だ。温めることで香味がまろやかに膨らみ、米の甘み旨みが伸びるようにあふれ出る。酸の押し出しも強く、食欲をそそる食中酒だ。

You can enjoy enhancement of flavor by warming the sake which is called Kan-agari. By warming it up, the aroma and taste are enhanced mellowly and the sweetness and savory of rice comes out steadily. Sourness also pushes the taste and the sake stimulates your appetite.

甘辛度
Sweet-dryness

甘　　　　　辛
Sweet　　　Dry

味わい
Taste

淡麗　　　　濃醇
Light　　　　Rich

香り
Aroma

低　　　　　高
Weak　　　Strong

原料米 華吹雪
酵母 非公開　アルコール度数 16　日本酒度 ±0
酸度 1.5　精米歩合 55%　小売価格 1262円　720ml
Raw material rice: Hana Fubuki
Yeast: Closed　Alcohol content: 16
Sake meter value: ±0　Acidity: 1.5
Rice-polishing rate: 55%　Retail price: 1262yen/720ml

Basic of sake-making is Junmai-shu
酒造りの基本は純米酒

「田酒」の名は酒の元となる田圃を意味し、日本の田圃で獲れる生産物のみを使用した、米の旨味が生きる純米酒が基本だ。「原点に返り、風格ある本物の酒造り」をコンセプトに昭和49年以来、昔ながらの完全な手造りで醸されている。米の旨みを追求するため、麹造りは常に最新のデータ分析に基づくものだ。

"Denshu" is named after rice fields which produce the ingredients of sake. Pure-rice sake with the full savory of rice is made only with products by Japanese rice fields. The brewery's concept is "to go back to basics and make real and stately sake". Since Showa 49 (1974), the brewery has making sake completely by hand. Koji is always made based on the latest data analysis to pursue the savory of rice.

撮影／名智健二

Enjoyable color of natural sake
酒本来の色も楽しめる

蔵の創業は明治11年（1878）。八甲田山系の軟水の伏流水で仕込まれた酒は、今では当たり前である活性炭を使った濾過をしていない。やや黄色く色づいているが、それが本来の酒の色だという。青森市にある蔵の前には、松前藩が参勤交代として通ったという松前街道も走る。

The brewery was founded in Meiji 11 (1878). This sake made with soft river-bed water from Hakkodasan mountains is not filtrated with activated charcoal which is regularly done nowadays. Therefore, the sake is naturally yellowish. In front of the brewery at Aomori-shi, there is Matsumae road which the domain lord of Matsumae used to attend Edo on duty.

NISHIDA Sake Brewery　西田酒造店

🏠 〒038-0059 青森県青森市油川大浜46　☎ 017-788-0007　酒蔵見学 不可　URL http://www.densyu.co.jp/
Add: 46 Aburakawaohama Aomori-shi, Aomori 038-0059　**Tel:** +81-17-788-0007　**Brewery tour:** NO　**URL:** http://www.densyu.co.jp/

NANBUBIJIN

Special Junmai-shu / 南部美人 特別純米酒

Iwate / 岩手

Finally made the ultimate sake for meals

ついに完成した究極の食中酒

岩手県オリジナルの酒造好適米「ぎんおとめ」を使用。きれいなふわっとした香り、ぽってりした米の甘みと旨みが充分に感じられ、のどにすっと落ちていく。飲み干したあとの豊かな余韻もいい。冷やでも燗でも楽しめる。

Sake-making rice, Ginotome made in Iwate prefecture is used. You can enjoy clean, light aroma and full sweetness and savory of rice with smoothness on your throat. Rich aftertaste is also good. You can enjoy it either chilled or warmed.

甘辛度
Sweet-dryness

甘　　　辛
Sweet　　　Dry

味わい
Taste

淡麗　　　濃醇
Light　　　Rich

香り
Aroma

低　　　高
Weak　　　Strong

原料米 ぎんおとめ（麹米/50%、掛米/55%）
酵母 M310、9号系酵母　アルコール度数 15〜16　日本酒度 +4
酸度 1.5　精米歩合 55%　小売価格 1500円 720ml
Raw material rice: Ginotome
Yeast: M310, Kobo no.9　Alcohol content: 15-16%
Sake meter value: +4　Acidity: 1.5
Rice-polishing rate: 55%　Retail price: 1500yen/720ml

Craftmanship of Nanbu Toji speaks
南部杜氏の技が冴える

様々な料理に合う「究極の食中酒」を目指して醸された。日本三大杜氏の筆頭に数えられる南部杜氏の技と伝統を受け継ぎ、吟醸酒と同じように低温発酵でじっくりと仕込んでいるので、デリケートな香りや繊細で複雑な味わいも加わり贅沢な仕上がりになっている。

The brewery creates this sake targeting "ultimate sake matches with meal" to enjoy with various kinds of dishes. Techniques and tradition of Nanbu (northern) brew master which is considered as the top of Japanese three greatest brew masters are taken over and this sake is made slowly with low temperature fermentation same as Ginjo-shu. Therefore, the taste is luxury with delicate aroma and subtle, complicated flavor.

Local sake of Ninohe (rice, water and people)
二戸（米、水、人）の地酒

蔵の創業は明治35年（1902）。仕込み水は二戸市の景勝地・折爪馬仙境峡の伏流水で、ミネラル分を豊富に含む酒造りに最適の中硬水だ。この名水、二戸産の酒米、地元・南部杜氏の技で醸された酒は、IWCのSAKE部門で最高賞「チャンピオン・サケ」に輝いた。

The brewery was founded in Meiji 35 (1902). River-bed water used for this sake is from scenic Orizumeba senkyo of Ninohe-shi and a middle hard water which contains rich mineral and suitable for sake-making. This sake created by excellent water, rice for sake made in Ninohe and a technique by local Nanbu brew master won "Champion Sake" which is the top honor of Sake division of IWC.

NANBU BIJIN Sake　南部美人

住 〒028-6101　岩手県二戸市福岡字上町13　☎ 0195-23-3133　酒蔵見学 可（冬季限定11月〜3月午後のみ　土日祝休　見学料1000円・試飲あり、おみやげ付き　詳細は☎かHP）　URL https://www.nanbubijin.co.jp/

Add: 13 Kami-machi, Fukuoka, Ninohe-shi, Iwate 028-6101　**Tel:** +81-195-23-3133　**Brewery tour:** YES (Only afternoon November -March except Sat, Sun and holidays, admission fee with tasting and souvenir. 1000 yen. For the details, call or visit HP below.)　**URL:** https://www.nanbubijin.co.jp/en/

HIROKI

Special Junmai-shu / 飛露喜 特別純米

Fukushima / 福島

Tongues are excited by the miracle taste!

奇跡の旨さに舌もお祭り騒ぎ!

日本酒の大人気銘柄のひとつであり、花香
のような上立ち香はあくまで穏やか。舌の
上で転がすと、マスカットのような甘い味
わいと奥深い旨みが広がり、思わず「旨い」
と唸るほどの高い独創性と完成度を誇る。

One of very popular Japanese sake with gentle floral top-note aroma. By sipping it, sweet taste like muscats and deep flavor fill in your mouth and makes you say, "It's good!" with its high originality and maturity.

甘辛度
Sweet-dryness

甘 —————●——— 辛
Sweet   Dry

味わい
Taste

淡麗 —————●——— 濃醇
Light   Rich

香り
Aroma

低 —————●——— 高
Weak   Strong

原料米 麹米/山田錦50%・掛米/五百万石55%
酵母 協会酵母9号・10号ブレンド **アルコール度数** 16.3 **日本酒度** +3
酸度 1.4 **精米分合** 55% **小売価格** 2600円 1800mlのみ
Raw material rice: Koji rice: Yamada Nishiki Rice-polishing rate: 50
Kake rice: Gohyakumangoku Rice-polishing rate: 55
Yeast: Kyokai Kobo no9 and 10 blend **Alcohol content:** 16.3%
Sake meter value: +3 **Acidity:** 1.4
Rice-polishing rate: 55% **Retail price:** 2600yen/1800ml only

Remove bran completely
糠は徹底的に洗い取る

蔵では原料処理に徹底的にこだわる。洗米は少量の米に分け、雑味の元になる糠を完全に取り去る。そして秒単位での水分管理を行い、外硬内軟のさばけのいい蒸米に仕上げる。でき上がった醪は温度管理ができる高性能タンクで、低温長期発酵させて醸すという。

The brewery prepares the ingredients with the greatest care. Rice is divided into small portions and remove bran completely to avoid bitterness. Moisture control by seconds makes not sticky, steamed rice which is soft inside. Moromi is fermented at low temperature for many hours in a high-performance tank which is capable to control temperature.

The president of the company is the brew master
社長が杜氏の酒造り

蔵の創業は江戸時代後期の文化文政年間(1804〜1830)。仕込み水は阿賀川の伏流水を使用しており、口当たりの優しい軟水だ。社長自ら杜氏として常に新しい酒造りを目指す姿勢は、若い蔵元杜氏からも熱く支持される。JALでは国際線ファーストクラスの酒として早くから提供され、外国人からの評価も高い。

The brewery was founded in Bunka-bunsei era, the late Edo period (1804-1830). Mild textured, riverbed water from Aga river is used for sake. The president of the company is the brew master who always tries to make a new sake, and popular among young generation brewers. It has been serving at first class of JAL international flights and popular among foreign people.

HIROKI SHUZO HONTEN　廣木酒造本店

〒969-6543 福島県河沼郡会津坂下町字市中二番甲3574　☎ 0242-83-2104 (不定休)　酒蔵見学 不可
Add: 3574 Ichinakanibanko, Aizubange-machi, Kawanuma-gun, Fukushima 969-6543　**Tel:** +81-242-83-2104 (irregular holiday)　**Brewery tour:** NO

YAMAHAI JUNMAI YUKINOBOSHA

Junmai-shu ／ 山廃純米 雪の茅舎

Akita ／ 秋田

Microorganism work on sake

微生物たちの力が酒に宿る

穏やかで微かに甘い吟醸香、しっとりした口当たり。山廃ならではのきめ細やかな酸味と米の濃醇な味わいのバランスも絶妙で、飲み口の切れの良さと旨みの余韻も楽しめる。燗にすると甘酸っぱい旨みが膨らむ。

Mild and slightly sweet Ginjo fruity aroma, and dewy texture. Yamahai's unique fine acid and rich full taste of rice are well-balanced, and you can also enjoy its sharpness and after-taste. By warming it up, sweet-sour flavor is enhanced.

甘辛度
Sweet-dryness

甘 ——————— 辛
Sweet   Dry

味わい
Taste

淡麗 ——————— 濃醇
Light   Rich

香り
Aroma

低 ——————— 高
Weak   Strong

アルコール分 16 度
原材料名 米（国産）・米麹（国産米）
精米歩合 65 ％

原料米 麹米／山田錦　掛米／秋田酒こまち
酵母 自家培養酵母　アルコール度数 15.6　日本酒度 +1.2
酸度 1.6　精米分合 65%　小売価格 1200円 720ml
Raw material rice: Koji rice: Yamada Nishiki　Kake rice: Akitasake Komachi　Yeast: Self-cultured Kobo　Alcohol content: 15.6%
Sake meter value: +1.2　Acidity: 1.6
Rice-polishing rate: 65%　Retail price: 1200yen/720ml

Sake-making by natural function
自然の働きにまかせた酒造り

蔵人たちの手で秋田酒こまちを栽培し、酒造りに向いた酒米作りの研究を続けている。造りでは、酵母の自家培養や山廃造りの復活とともに、「櫂入れしない」「濾過しない」「割水しない」の3無い造りで醸される。酵母の自然の働きにまかせ、搾ったままのおいしい状態を保つためだ。

Akita-shu Komachi is grown by brewery workers. The brewery has been pursuing study of rice farming suitable for sake-making. With revival of self-culture of Kobo and Yamahai making, the sake is made without Kaiire (mixing Moromi), filtration and Warimizu (added water before bottling). This allows for Kobo being natural and keeping the taste as it was pressed.

Smoothly soft water for sake-making tastes good
仕込み水は飲んでも旨い超軟水

蔵の創業は明治35年（1902）。蔵のある由利本荘市石脇地区は、水の恵み豊かな地。仕込み水に使う蔵内に出る湧水は、舌を滑らすほど超軟水で旨い。蔵は精米所が高く、続いて仕込蔵、貯蔵の蔵とつながる高低差6mの地形にあり、「のぼり蔵」と呼ばれ明治・大正の面影を残す。

The brewery was founded in Meiji 35 (1902). The brewery is at Ishiwaki district of Yurihonjo-shi abundant in water from Chokai mountain. Water sprung in the brewery used for sake-making is smoothly soft and tastes good. In the brewery, a rice milling room is set at the highest place. Toward lower areas, a fermentation room and then storage room are located on a 6 meters-height different slope. It is called "Nobori-kura" which has been employed during Meiji and Taisho era.

SAIYA SHUZOUTEN　齋彌酒造店

🏠 〒015-0011秋田県由利本荘市石脇字石脇53　☎ 0184-22-0536　**酒蔵見学** 可（1週間前に要予約　土日祝、年末年始、盆は休み）
URL http://www.yukinobosha.jp/
Add: 53 Ishiwaki aza Ishiwaki, Yurihonjo-city, Akita 015-0011　**Tel:** +81-184-22-0536　**Brewery tour:** YES (reservation required one week prior to visit. Closed on Sat, Sun, holidays, new years and Bon holidays)　**URL:** http://www.yukinobosha.jp/

KIKUHIME TSURUNOSATO

Junmai-shu / 菊姫 鶴乃里

ishikawa / 石川

"Kikusake of Kaga" loved by Toyotomi Hideyoshi

豊臣秀吉も愛した「加賀の菊酒」

安土桃山時代より、美酒「加賀の菊酒」として誉高い。ほのかに甘い香り、やわらかな舌ざわりのあと上品できれいな旨みが広がる。続いて山廃ならではの酸味が、味わいに豊かさと力強さを絡ませ、後の切れもいい。

Since Azuchi-Momoyama era, it has been prestigious as an excellent sake "Kikuhime of Kaga". Slightly sweet aroma and mild texture are followed by refined, clean taste. Subsequently, Yamahai's unique sourness adds richness and strength to the taste and the aftertaste is sharp.

甘辛度 Sweet-dryness	
甘 Sweet	辛 Dry

味わい Taste	
淡麗 Light	濃醇 Rich

香り Aroma	
低 Weak	高 Strong

原料米 山田錦
酵母 山廃酵母　アルコール度数 16度以上17度未満　日本酒度 非公開
酸度 非公開　精米歩合 65%　小売価格 2000円 720ml
Raw material rice: Yamada Nishiki
Yeast: Yamahai Kobo　Alcohol content: 16-16.9%
Sake meter value: Closed　Acidity: Closed
Rice-polishing rate: 65%　Retail price: 2000yen/720ml

Revival of traditional Yama-hai zukuri
日本伝統の山廃造りを復活

菊姫では搾った酒を熟成させ、適熟になるまで寝かせている。この酒も冬の厳寒期に造り、蔵内でひと夏ゆっくり熟成させることで新酒独特の荒さが消え、なめらかな落ち着いた味わいに仕上がる。蔵では昭和50年代から山廃造りも復活。濃醇で飲み応えのある山廃仕込みの酒は、鴨肉の治部煮など旨みの強い料理によく合う。

The brewery matures pressed sake until it is aged properly. This sake is made during extreme cold winter and aged during summer. By this method, roughness of newly-made sake is removed, and smooth and mature taste is made. The brewery re-started Yamahai-zukuri from Showa 50s (around 1980). Rich and firm sake made with Yamahai matches well with a rich flavor dish such as duck meat Jibuni (simmered).

Sake-making from blessing from sacred Hakusan
霊峰白山の恵みで酒を醸す

蔵の創業は天正年間(1570～1600)。霊峰白山と手取川水系の自家井戸から汲み上げる仕込み水を使い、日本でもトップランクの山田錦で吟醸酒・純米酒を醸している。前には江戸時代に白山参拝で賑わった鶴来街道が走り、蔵界隈には旅心をそそる歴史ある門前町の風情が続く。

The brewery was founded in Tensho era (1570-1600). The brewery draws water from their own well originated from sacred Hakusan mountain and Tedori river and uses top-ranked domestic rice Yamada Nishiki for their Ginjo-shu and Junmai-shu making. There is Tsurugi road people used to visit Hakusan in Edo era in front of the brewery. A classical atmosphere of historical temple town around the brewery makes you want to visit the site.

KIKUHIME　菊姫

🏠 〒920-2126　石川県白山市鶴来新町タ8番地　☎ 076-272-1234　**酒蔵見学** 不可　**URL** http://www.kikuhime.co.jp/
Add: Ta8, Tsurugi-shinmachi, Hakusan-shi, Ishikawa 920-2126　**Tel:** +81-76-272-1234　**Brewery tour:** NO　**URL:** http://www.kikuhime.co.jp/

BORN JUNMAI55

Junmai-shu ／ 梵・純米55

Fukui ／ 福井

Aged more than a year at icy cold temperature

1年以上氷温でじっくり熟成

酒は米と米麹だけで醸す純米酒のみ。爽やか
な香りだが、口当たりのきれいさのあとで、
厚みのある旨み、奥に伸びる深い味わいが広
がってくる。後口の切れも素晴らしい。燗
にすると酸が効いてさらに味わいが深まる。

The brewery makes Junmai-shu made with
rice and koji of rice only. Clean texture is followed by thick flavor and deep taste fills in
your mouth. It has an excellent sharp aftertaste. By warming it, sourness comes out and
the taste becomes deeper.

甘辛度
Sweet-dryness

甘 ——————— 辛
Sweet   Dry

味わい
Taste

淡麗 ——————— 濃醇
Light   Rich

香り
Aroma

低 ——————— 高
Weak   Strong

原料米 山田錦・五百万石®
酵母 自社酵母　アルコール度数 15　日本酒度 非公開
酸度 非公開　精米歩合 55%　小売価格 1191円 720ml
Raw material rice: Yamada Nishiki, Gohyakumangoku
Yeast: Kobo made by the brewery　Alcohol content: 15%
Sake meter value: Closed　Acidity: Closed
Rice-polishing rate: 55%　Retail price: ¥1191/720ml

兵庫県特A地区産契約栽培山田錦・福井県産五百万石

Average rice-polishing rate of the brewery is about 34%
蔵内の平均精米歩合約34%

使用する原料米は山田錦と五百万石だけ。蔵内の平均精米歩合は約34％と、大吟醸の50％を大きく下回り、酒質のきれいさは群を抜いている。同時にマイナスの温度帯で最低でも1年、長いもので10年以上も氷温熟成させて、果実香となめらかさを際立たせている。福井名産の、くせの強いサバのへしこにも合う。

Only Yamada-Nishiki and Gohyakumangoku are used as the ingredient rice. Average rice-polishing rate of the brewery is about 34% which is way lower than 50% of Dai-ginjo, and the cleanness of sake quality is a top class. At the same time, it is matured in ice temperature for one year at least and 10 years at most to enhance fruity aroma and smoothness.

Playing classical music for sake-making
酒にクラシック音楽を聴かせる

蔵の創業は万延元年（1860）。仕込み水は、地下約184mからくみ上げた白山連邦の伏流水。完全冷却された吹き抜け5階建て、1年中極寒の環境で酒造りができる「天空蔵」も完成。酒にクラシック音楽を聴かせるなどの造りにも挑戦中だ。

The brewery was founded in Manen 1 (1860). Riverbed water drawn about 184 meters below ground from Hakusan mountains is used. In the property admiring the view of Hakusan, five-story "Tenku kura" which is capable to make sake under extreme cold environment all year round with complete cooling facility, is built. The brewery has been challenging a new method to play classical music for sake-making.

KATOUKICHIBEE SHOUTEN　加藤吉平商店 きちべえ

住 〒916-0001 福井県鯖江市吉江町1-11　電 0778-51-1507　酒蔵見学 原則不可（要相談）　URL http://www.born.co.jp/
Add: 1-11 Yoshie-cho, Sabae-shi, Fukui 916-0001 Japan　Tel: +81-778-51-1507　Brewery tour: In principle impossible (Consultation required)
URL: http://www.born.co.jp/

KIMOTO JUNMAI **OKUSHIKA** MUROKA NAMAGENSHU

Junmai-shu / 生酛純米 奥鹿 無濾過生原酒

Osaka / 大阪

Fertilizer and pesticide-free rice is used for sake-making

化学肥料・農薬無使用の酒米で醸す

熟成感のある複雑な香り、非常に味わい深い骨太な酒質は、他の日本酒とは一線を画す。無濾過生原酒の豊潤だが雑味のない旨み、自然界の乳酸菌を活用した生酛ならではの酸の強さなど、百花繚乱の香味を楽しもう。

Complicated, matured aroma and quite deep and steady sake quality is unique and different from other Japanese sake. Not filtrated, unpasteurized sake has rich taste without off-flavor. Let's enjoy varieties of aroma and taste such as sourness comes from Kimoto (starter culture) utilizes natural lactic acid bacteria.

甘辛度
Sweet-dryness

甘 — 辛
Sweet — Dry

味わい
Taste

淡麗 — 濃醇
Light — Rich

香り
Aroma

低 — 高
Weak — Strong

原料米 山田錦
酵母 協会7号　アルコール度数 18　日本酒度 +7
酸度 2.7　精米分合 60%　小売価格 2380円 720ml
Raw material rice: Yamada Nishiki
Yeast: Kyokai no.7　Alcohol content: 18%
Sake meter value: +7　Acidity: 2.7
Rice-polishing rate: 60%　Retail price: ¥2380/720ml

The brewery is sake-rice chateau
酒米シャトーを実践

昭和60年代より自営田で山田錦栽培に取り組み、現在では約17町歩の田すべてで、化学肥料・農薬無使用で栽培。米作りから酒造りまでを一貫して社員総出で実践する、酒米シャトーだ。酒造りも、酵母の働きを見守りながら進めるなど、自然の摂理を大切にしている。

From Showa 60s (around 1990), the brewery has been trying to grow Yamada Nishiki at their rice fields. Today, they grow fertilizer and pesticide-free rice at about 17 hectares of their rice fields. It is a sort of sake rice chateau since the brewery staff conduct consistent sake-making from rice farming. The brewery also values laws of nature, for example, to check the status of Kobo while making sake.

Aged until the best timing
飲み頃になるまで蔵で熟成

蔵の創業は明治19年 (1886)。仕込み水は蔵の裏にある歌垣山の伏流水で、昔から名水と謳われる軟水だ。名水で醸したあとは飲み頃になるまで熟成期間を設ける。この酒は10〜15度の低温で5年以上熟成させたという。

The brewery was founded in Meiji 19 (1886). The brewery uses river-bed water from Utagaki mountain behind the brewery which is soft and has been well-known since the old time. After sake is made with the water, it is matured until the best timing to drink. This sake is aged at 10-15 degrees of low temperature for more than 5 years.

AKISHIKA SHUZO　秋鹿酒造

〒563-0113 大阪府豊能郡能勢町倉垣1007　072-737-0013　酒蔵見学 不可
Add: 1007 Kuragaki, Nose-cho, Toyono-gun, Osaka 563-0113　**Tel:** +81-72-737-0013　**Brewery tour:** NO

NISHINOSEKI TEZUKURI JYUNMAI-SHU

Junmai-shu / 西の関 手造り純米酒

Oita ／大分

Hall of Fame Sake matches with Unagi

ウナギに合う酒として殿堂入り

香りはあくまで穏やかだが、口に含むと蒸米
のような甘みを感じる。旨みと酸味のバラ
ンスも良く、米本来の豊かな味わいが楽し
める。燗にするとさらに芳醇な旨みと、酸
の押し出しが効いて、後口の切れも増す。

The aroma is mild, but you can feel sweetness like a steamed rice when you sip it. The
flavor and sourness are well-balanced, and
you can enjoy rich taste of real rice. By warming it, richer flavor and sourness comes out
and the aftertaste becomes sharper.

| 甘辛度 Sweet-dryness |
| 甘 ——————●—— 辛 |
| Sweet · · · · · · · Dry |

| 味わい Taste |
| 淡麗 ——————●—— 濃醇 |
| Light · · · · · · · Rich |

| 香り Aroma |
| 低 ————●———— 高 |
| Weak · · · · · · · Strong |

原料米 麹米／八反錦　掛米／ヒノヒカリ
酵母 協会901号　アルコール度数 15　日本酒度 −1.5
酸度 1.4　精米分合 60%　小売価格 1140円 720ml
Raw material rice: Koji rice: Hattan Nishiki　Kake rice: Hinohikari
Yeast: Kyokai Kobo no.901　**Alcohol content:** 15%
Sake meter value: -1.5　**Acidity:** 1.4
Rice-polishing rate: 60%　**Retail price:** ¥1140/720ml

Sake-making begins with cleaning
酒造りは掃除から始まる

酒蔵の良し悪しは蔵の清潔感に比例するというが、蔵内にはごみひとつなく、古い蔵の床もピカピカだ。大分県の地元に根差したおいしい酒造りが基本だが、酒団体主催のウナギに合う日本酒のNO.1に11年連続で輝き、12年目に殿堂入り。料理を引き立てる銘酒として、全国にもファンが多い。

It is said cleanliness shows whether the brewery is good or bad. Tools for cleaning the brewery and tanks are hand-made with bamboos and bamboo grasses from old times. The brewery basically makes good sake locally in Oita prefecture, but it has been selected as the best matching sake with Unagi eel by an organization of sake for 12 years in a row and has many fans all over Japan as an excellent sake to match with meals.

Sake from home of Shugen-do
修験道の里の酒

蔵の創業は明治6年(1873)。仕込み水は国東半島の山からの伏流水。軽やかで非常にやわらかく甘みもあり、酒質の大きな源になっている。蔵のある国東半島は奈良・平安時代より神仏習合の山岳仏教が花開き、遺跡が多く残ることから「仏の里」とも呼ばれている。

The brewery was founded in Meiji 6 (1873). Riverbed water drawn from mountains of Kunisaki peninsula is used. This light, very mild, sweet water defines the quality of sake. The brewery is at Kunisaki peninsula which is called "Village of Buddha" since mountain Buddhism of Syncretization of Shinto with Buddhism is prospered from Nara-Heian era and many ruins still remain.

KAYASHIMA SAKE BREWING　萱島酒造

🏠 〒873-0513　大分県国東市国東町綱井392-1　☎ 0978-72-1181　酒蔵見学 可(要予約)　URL http://www.nishinoseki.com/
Add: 392-1, Kunisaki machi-Tsunai, Kunisaki-shi, Oita 873-0513　Tel: +81-978-72-1181　Brewery tour: YES (reservation required)　URL: http://www.nishinoseki.com/

Daiginjo-shu, Ginjo-shu, Honjozo-shu

大吟醸酒・吟醸酒・本醸造酒

　日本酒の香りは酵母の種類に由来する。果実のようなさまざまな香りは、活動できるギリギリの低温の環境下に置かれた酵母が身を守るために、体内にある酵素を使うことで生み出される香気成分によるものだ。ここでは、この吟醸造りを徹底的に管理して、高い酒質を誇る日本酒を紹介する。

Aroma of Japanese sake is determined by the types of Kobo. Various aroma like fruits come from aroma component produced using its enzyme to protect Kobo itself under low temperature environment which is the lowest limit for Kobo to be active. This section introduces Japanese sake proudly have high-quality created by through control of Ginjo making process.

KUZURYU DAIGINJO

Daiginjo-shu / 九頭龍 大吟醸

Fukui / 福井

Daiginjo for warming made by 5 years effort

5年の歳月をかけて完成した燗酒用大吟醸

大吟醸は通常は冷やして飲むが、燗酒用に造られた大吟醸だ。洋梨のような果実香、甘くやわらかい口当たり。温める前はきれいで淡麗だが、燗にするときれいさはそのままに、花開くように旨み甘みと味の幅が広がる。

Daiginjo-shu is commonly chilled, but this is made to warm. Fruity pear-like aroma and sweet, mild texture. Before warming, it is clean and light. Once it is warmed, it keeps the cleanliness, but the flavor, sweetness and taste become deeper like a blooming flower.

甘辛度 / Sweet-dryness
甘 Sweet ——— 辛 Dry

味わい / Taste
淡麗 Light ——— 濃醇 Rich

香り / Aroma
低 Weak ——— 高 Strong

原料米 国産酒造好適米
酵母 蔵内保存酵母　アルコール度数 15　日本酒度 +5.5
酸度 1.0　精米分合 50%　小売価格 2500円 720ml
Raw material rice: Sake brewering rice made in Japan
Yeast: Savedyeast at Warehouse.　**Alcohol content:** 15%
Sake meter value: +5.5　**Acidity:** 1.0
Rice-polishing rate: 50%　**Retail price:** 2500yen/720ml

Ginjo brewery represents Hokuriku area
北陸きっての吟醸蔵

昭和50年にいち早く大吟醸「龍」を発売するなど、北陸きっての吟醸蔵。くせのないきれいな酒質は、米や水、原料処理や熟成など様々な研究を重ねてきた賜物である。この酒はさらに麹の状態から酒造りに至るまで、温度管理や熟成期間を徹底的に研究。5年の歳月をかけて完成した、技術の粋を結晶した燗用酒だ。

The brewery of Ginjo-shu represents Hokuriku area which releases Daiginjo "Ryu" in Showa 50 (1975) which was early among the market. The plain and clean quality is made by studying efforts of rice, water, ingredient preparation and aging. Moreover, temperature control and aging period from status of Koji through sake-making are thoroughly studied. This sake for warming is, so to speak, made by completed technologies of 5 years effort.

Close to Eiheiji, zen temple
禅寺・永平寺も近い

蔵の創業は文化元年 (1804)。仕込み水は、霊峰白山の雪解け水を源流とする、蔵近くを流れる九頭竜川の伏流水。やわらかく軽いしなやかな口当たりは、きれいで膨らみのある吟醸酒造りに最適という。「黒龍」の名も九頭竜川の古い呼び名である。福井名産の、繊細で旨みの濃い越前ガニとの相性も抜群だ。

The brewery was founded in Bunka 1st (1804). Riverbed water from Kuzuryu river runs near the brewery and originated from snowmelt from sacred Hakusan mountain, is used. Mild, light and silky texture of water is suitable for clean and mellow Ginjo-shu. "Kokuryu" is an old name of Kuzuryu river. It matches well with Fukui's specialty, delicate and rich-flavored Echizen crabs.

KOKURYU Sake Brewing   黒龍酒造

🏠 〒910-1133　福井県吉田郡永平寺町松岡春日1-38　☎ 0776-61-6110　酒蔵見学 不可　URL http://www.kokuryu.co.jp/
Add: 1-38 Matsuoka kasuga, Eiheiji-cho, Yoshida-gun, Fukui 910-1133　**Tel:** +81-776-61-6110　**Brewery tour:** NO　**URL:** http://www.kokuryu.co.jp/en/

GINJO ISOJIMAN

Ginjo-shu / 吟醸 磯自慢

Shizuoka / 静岡

Juicy, treasured Ginjo-shu

瑞々しさいっぱい、至宝の吟醸酒

リンゴのようなほのかな果実香、アルコール
をまったく感じさせないやわらかい口当たり
と、爽快でまるい味わい。口の中で転がすと、
瑞々しいきれいな甘みと旨みが広がりスッと
消える。崇高なる透明感に満ちた逸品だ。

Apple-like delicate fruity aroma, mild texture
tastes like non-alcohol and refreshing, round-
ed flavor. When you have it in your mouth,
juicy, clean sweetness and flavor fill in your
mouth and disappear. It is an excellent sake
filled with sublime transparency.

甘辛度
Sweet-dryness
甘　　　　辛
Sweet　　　Dry

味わい
Taste
淡麗　　　濃醇
Light　　　Rich

香り
Aroma
低　　　　高
Weak　　Strong

原料米 山田錦※　**酵母** 自社保存酵母
アルコール度数 15度以上16度未満　**日本酒度** +6〜+7　**酸度** 1.1
精米歩合 麹50%　掛米55%　**小売価格** 3450円 1800mlのみ
Raw material rice: Yamada Nishiki　Yeast: Kobo stored by the
brewery　Alcohol content: 15-15.9%　Sake meter value: +6-+7
Acidity: 1.1　Rice-polishing rate: Koji 50% Kake rice 55%
Retail price: ¥3450/1800ml only

※特A地区東条産 山田錦

Matches perfectly with seafoods
魚介には最高に合う

質の高い酒造りを志し、吟醸酒の旨さを全国に
知らしめたスター的存在の蔵。最高品質の山田
錦を使い、大量の水を使った限定吸水による原
料処理、手造りの磯自慢流麹造りと吟醸用の酒
母造り、低温発酵での醪管理、昔ながらの酒袋
による搾りと、工程すべてに心血を注ぐ。

Aiming at making a high-quality sake, this star
brewery let people nationwide know the taste of
Ginjo-shu. Using top-quality Yamada Nishiki, the
raw materials are prepared in limited water absorp-
tion rice washing with a great amount of water. The
brewery also makes its original koji and shubo
(starter culture) for Ginjo. Moreover, moromi (fermentation mash) is controlled in low temperature
and a cloth bag is traditionally used for pressing
stage. They devote heart and soul to every process.

Always winter in the brewery
蔵内は常に真冬の環境

蔵の創業は天保元年 (1830)。仕込み水は南アル
プス間ノ岳を源泉とする大井川の伏流水で、飲
んでも旨い軟水だ。蔵のある焼津は冬でも温暖
なため、常に真冬の環境を保てるステンレスの
冷蔵仕込み蔵で醸される。でき上がった酒はす
べて5度以下の低温冷蔵庫で管理熟成を行うの
も吟醸蔵ならでは。

The brewery was founded in Tenpo 1 (1830). Riverbed water from Ooi river originated from Ainoda-
ke mountain of Southern Alps is used for sake
making. The water is soft and tastes good. The
brewery is at Yaizu which is warm in winter, therefore, sake is made in cold, stainless kura (storage).
Since it is Ginjo-kura, all of made sake are stored
and aged in a refrigerator lower then 5 degrees.

ISOJIMAN Sake Brewing　磯自慢酒造

[住] 〒425-0032静岡県焼津市鰯ヶ島307　[TEL] 054-628-2204　[酒蔵見学] 不可　[URL] http://www.isojiman-sake.jp/
Add: 307 Iwashi-ga-shima, Yaizu City, Shizuoka 425-0032　**Tel:** +81-54-628-2204　**Brewery tour:** NO　**URL:** http://www.isojiman-sake.jp/
en/

KAIUN GINJO

Ginjo-shu / 開運 吟醸

Shizuoka／静岡

Ginjo-shu taken over the craftmanship

能登四天王杜氏の技が息づく吟醸酒

爽やかで瑞々しくきれいな酒質にこだわる、蔵の思いが籠る酒だ。梨のような穏やかな吟醸香で苦みや渋みを感じさせず、舌にすっと吸い込まれるような軽やかな飲み口。爽快感あふれる旨さで、切れの良さも素晴らしい。

This sake is made by the brewery pursues refreshing, juicy and clean quality. Pear-like, mild Ginjo aroma. Light texture absorbed on your tongue without any bitterness and astringency. It has a full of refreshing taste and wonderful sharp aftertaste.

甘辛度
Sweet-dryness

甘　　　　辛
Sweet　　　Dry

味わい
Taste

淡麗　　　濃醇
Light　　　Rich

香り
Aroma

低　　　　高
Weak　　　Strong

原料米 山田錦
酵母 静岡酵母　アルコール度数 16度以上17度未満　日本酒度 +5
酸度 1.3　精米歩合 50%　小売価格 1600円 720ml
Raw material rice: Yamada Nishiki
Yeast: Shizuoka Kobo　Alcohol content: 16-16.9%
Sake meter value: +5　Acidity: 1.3
Rice-polishing rate: 50%　Retail price: 1600yen/720ml

Key brewery made Shizuoka Ginjo famous
静岡吟醸発信の立役者

最高級の酒米山田錦をふんだんに使い、能登四天王杜氏として名声を馳せた波瀬正吉氏の技の伝承と、高品質の酒造りへの設備投資をいち早く進め、吟醸酒造りを確立。静岡全土にも広げ、静岡吟醸の全国発信を牽引した蔵として名高い。大吟醸と同じく、長期低温発酵させた醪で醸している。

Using Yamada Nishiki, a top-class sake rice, Ginjo sake making is established with the technique of the late Shokichi Hase who was famous as one of Noto greatest brew master and equipment investment for high-quality sake making. It is spread to all over Shizuoka and known as the leading brewery of Shizuoka Ginjo to be popular nationwide. As same as Daiginjo, moromi (fermentation mash) is fermented at low temperature for a long term.

Eco-friendly sake-making
環境にも優しい酒造り

蔵の創業は明治5年(1872)。仕込み水には蔵近くの高天神城跡から湧き出る軟水を使用。軟水だが発酵に強く、酒造りには最適だ。蔵には雑排水を浄化する大型排水処理施設や、太陽電池パネルを屋根に敷き詰めた大型冷蔵倉庫もあり、環境に優しい酒造りに取り組む。

The brewery was founded in Meiji 5 (1872). Soft water drawn from Takatenjin Castle Ruins near the brewery is used. It is soft, but strong against fermentation, so it is suitable for sake-making. The brewery is eco-friendly installing a large effluent treatment facility to purify discharged water and a large chilled storage room activated by solar battery panel on its roof.

DOI BREWERY　土井酒造場

🏠 〒437-1407静岡県掛川市小貫633　☎ 0537-74-2006　酒蔵見学 不可　URL http://kaiunsake.com/
Add: 633 Konuki, Kakegawa-shi, Shizuoka 437-1407　**Tel:** +81-537-74-2006　**Brewery tour:** NO　**URL:** http://kaiunsake.com/english

JUYONDAI HONMARU HIDEN TAMAGAESHI

Ginjo-shu / 吟醸酒 十四代 本丸 秘伝玉返し

Yamagata / 山形

Popular, top-brand made by brew owner

蔵元杜氏が造る最高峰の人気銘柄

平成6年に彗星の如く現れて以来、常に最高峰の人気銘柄。華やかで上品な吟醸香、口に含むと洋梨のような瑞々しさと旨みが弾けるようだ。最後は透明感のある綺麗で淡麗な味わいが、糸を引くように余韻に残る。

Since the brewery had appeared like a comet in Heisei 6 (1994), it is always a popular, top-brand. The sake has a bright and refined Ginjo aroma and juicy, pear-like flavor bursts into your mouth. Finally, transparent, clean and subtle taste remains long but delicate.

甘辛度
Sweet-dryness
甘　　　辛
Sweet　　Dry

味わい
Taste
淡麗　　　濃醇
Light　　Rich

香り
Aroma
低　　　高
Weak　　Strong

日本酒
原材料名／米・米麹
醸造アルコール
精米歩合 55%
アルコール分15度　1.8ℓ詰
国産米100%使用
お酒は20歳になってから。

製造年月

原料米 麹米／山田錦・出羽燦々
酵母 非公開　**アルコール度数** 15　**日本酒度** 非公開
酸度 非公開　**精米歩合** 55%　**小売価格** 2000円 1800mlのみ
Raw material rice: Yamada Nishiki, Dewa sansan
Yeast: Closed　Alcohol content: 15%
Sake meter value: Closed　Acidity: Closed
Rice-polishing rate: 55%　Retail price: 2000yen/1800ml only

Keeps challenging new sake-making
絶えず新しい酒造りに挑戦

淡麗辛口の酒が主流の時代に、華やかな香りとフレッシュな味わい、濃醇な旨みで一躍ブレイク。蔵元杜氏の寵児として後進に大きな影響を与え、多くの若い蔵元が杜氏として新しい酒造りを目指すきっかけとなった。山田錦を始め、雄町、愛山、自社開発の酒米、自社の蔵付酵母などの新しい酒造りに挑戦している。

In the time of light and dry sake, the sake becomes popular for its bright aroma, fresh taste and rich flavor. The revolutionary of sake brew master gave a big influence on young generations and many young brew workers decided to be a brew master. The brewery does not settle for the popularity and has been challenging a new sake-making using self-developed sake rice such as Yamada Nishiki, Omachi and Aiyama, and Kura's own Kobo.

Natural spring water in the brewery
蔵内には湧水場もある

蔵の創業は元和元年（1615）。仕込み水は葉山山系を水源とする自然湧水。蔵内の桜の老木の下から湧き出ており「桜清水」と呼ばれる。このまろやかな水質から生まれた、今までなかった芳醇旨口という新ジャンルの美酒には、地元名産の糖度の高いアスパラガス料理などがおすすめだ。

The brewery was founded in Genna 1 (1615). Natural spring water from Hayama mountains is used. The water sprung under an old cherry tree in the brewery is called "Sakura Shimizu (clear water from a cherry tree)". For this rich and sweet sake which is new and sensational, a local special asparagus which has a high sugar content is recommended.

TAKAGI SHUZO　高木酒造

🏠 〒995-0208山形県村山市大字富並1826　☎ 0237-57-2131　酒蔵見学 不可
Add: 1826 Oaza Tominami, Murayama-shi, Yamagata 995-0208　**Tel:** +81-237-57-2131　**Brewery tour:** NO

Non-premium, aged, cloudy, sparkling and wooden-bucket prepared sake

普通酒・古酒・にごり酒・ スパークリング日本酒・木桶仕込みの酒

いま市場には、さまざまなジャンルの日本酒が登場している。普通酒でも質の高いものが増え、にごり酒やスパークリング日本酒はアルコール分5%〜15%までと幅広い。古酒や木桶仕込みの酒には、シェリーなどのように味わい深いものもある。ここでは、そんな多彩なジャンルの日本酒を紹介する。

There are various kinds of Japanese sake on the market. Many of non-premium sake are high-quality, and cloudy sake and sparkling sake vary from 5% to 15% in alcohol content. Some aged sake and wooden-bucket prepared sake taste deep like shelly. This section introduces various kinds of Japanese sake.

HOURAI TEMSAITOJINO NYUKONSHU

Non-Premiun Sake / 蓬莱　天才杜氏の入魂酒

Gufu／岐阜

普通酒と秘蔵吟醸酒を、黄金比率でブレンド。やわらかな甘みと澄んだ味わい、燗にすると甘酸っぱい旨みも広がり、地元料理の飛騨牛の朴葉味噌焼きに合う。

Non-premium and treasured Ginjo-shu are blended in golden ratio. It has a mild sweetness and clear taste. By warming, sour and sweet flavor fills in your mouth. It matches with grilled Hida beef with Hoba miso.

蔵の創業は明治3年(1870)。IWCではコストパフォーマンスに最も優れた酒に選ばれた。

The brewery was founded in Meiji 3 (1870). It won the great value champion sake of IWC.

甘辛度
Sweet-dryness
甘　　　　辛
Sweet　　　　Dry

味わい
Taste
淡麗　　　　濃醇
Light　　　　Rich

香り
Aroma
低　　　　高
Weak　　　　Strong

原料米 ひだほまれ
酵母 非公開　アルコール度数 15
日本酒度 +2　酸度 1.5　精米分合 68%
小売価格 838円 720ml
Raw material rice: Hidahomare
Yeast: Closed　Alcohol content: 15%
Sake meter value: +2　Acidity: 1.5
Rice-polishing rate: 68%
Retail price: 838yen/720ml

WATANABE Shuzo-ten　渡辺酒造店

所 〒509-4234　岐阜県飛騨市古川町壱之町 7-7
☎ 0577-73-0012　酒蔵見学 可（詳細は電話またはホームページにて。要予約）URL http://www.sake-hourai.co.jp/
Add: 7-7 Ichinomachi, Furukawa-cho, Hida-shi, Gifu 509-4234
Tel: +81-577-73-0012　Brewery tour: YES (For details, call or see HP below. Reservation required)　URL: http://www.sake-hourai.co.jp/

HANAHATO

KIJOSHU AGED FOR 8 YEARS

Aged Kijo-shu / 華鳩　貴醸酒　8年貯蔵

Hiroshima ／広島

貴醸酒とは、水と清酒で醸した酒で、トロ
リと甘く濃厚な旨みを持つ。それを常温の
蔵で8年以上貯蔵。鴨のローストやバニラ
アイスにかけても旨い。

Kijo-shu is made with sake other than water.
It has a sweet, thick and rich flavor. It is stored
in room temperature storage more than 8
years. It tastes good putting on a roasted
duck or vanilla ice cream.

蔵の創業は明治32年(1899)。樽
貯蔵酒や20年古酒もある。

The brewery was founded in
Meiji 32 (1899). There are also
cask storage sake and 20years
old sake.

甘辛度
Sweet-dryness

甘 ———————— 辛
Sweet　　　　Dry

味わい
Taste

淡麗 ———————— 濃醇
Light　　　　Rich

香り
Aroma

低 ———————— 高
Weak　　　　Strong

原料米 こしひかり、中生新千本など食米
酵母 協会7号　**アルコール度数** 16
日本酒度 −44　**酸度** 3.5　**精米分合** 65〜
70%　**小売価格** 2000円 500ml
Raw material rice:
Koshihikari,Nakateshinsenbon etc.
Yeast: Kyokai No7　Alcohol content: 16%
Sake meter value: -44　Acidity: 3.5
Rice-polishing rate: 65-70%　Retail
price: 2000yen/500ml

ENOKI Shuzo　榎酒造

所 〒 737-1205　広島県呉市音戸町南隠渡 2-1-15
☎ 0823-52-1234　**酒蔵見学** 可（要予約）
URL http://hanahato.ocnk.net/
Add: 2-1-15 Minami-ondo, Ondo-cho, Kure-shi, Hiroshima.
737-1205　**Tel:** +81-823-52-1234　**Brewery tour:** YES (reservation
required)　**URL:** http://hanahato.ocnk.net/

TSUKINOKATSURA

Honjozo / 月の桂 大極上中汲にごり酒 本醸造

Kyoto ／ 京都

日本で最初（昭和39年）の発売時から人気を博し続ける、米のスパークリングともいえる元祖にごり酒。自然の炭酸ガスを含む果実香のある爽快な味わいは、食中酒にも向く。

From its release in Showa 39 (1964), this original cloudy sake which can be called rice champagne has been popular. Refreshing taste with fruity note containing natural carbon dioxide matches with meals.

蔵の創業は延宝3年(1675)。仕込水は伏見の伏流水で和釜で蒸す。

The brewery was founded in Enpo 3 (1675).Riverbed water from Katsura river is used and rice is steamed with Japanese cauldron.

甘辛度
Sweet-dryness
甘　　　　辛
Sweet　　　Dry

味わい
Taste
淡麗　　　　濃醇
Light　　　Rich

香り
Aroma
低　　　　高
Weak　　　Strong

原料米 麹米／五百万石　掛米／京の輝き
酵母 協会701　アルコール度数 17
日本酒度 -1～+1　酸度 1.5
精米分合 60%　小売価格 1300円 720ml
Raw material rice: Koji rice Gohyakumangoku Kake rice Kyo no Kagayaki　Yeast: Kyokai 701　Alcohol content: 17%　Sake meter value: -1~+1 Acidity: 1.5　Rice-polishing rate: 60% Retail price: 1300yen/720ml

MASUDA TOKUBEE Shoten　増田德兵衞商店

所 〒612-8471　京都市伏見区下鳥羽長田町135
☎ 075-611-5151 (9:00-17:00)　酒蔵見学 不可
URL https://www.tsukinokatsura.co.jp/ec_shop/
Add: 135 Shimotoba Osada-cho, Fushimi-ku, Kyoto-shi, Kyoto 612-8471　Tel: +81-75-611-5151 (9am-5pm)　Brewery tour: NO
URL: https://www.tsukinokatsura.co.jp/ec_shop/

ICHINOKURA SPARKLING SAKE SUZUNE

Sparkling／一ノ蔵 発泡清酒 すず音

Miyagi／宮城

スパークリング清酒の草分けで、1998 年に発売。きめ細かい泡は舌に優しく、新鮮な果実のような香りとやわらかな甘酸っぱさは、酒肴なしでも楽しめる。

It is a pioneer of sparkling sake which was released on 1998. Fine bubbles are tender on your tongue and you can enjoy the fresh fruity aroma and mild sweet-sourness without any snacks.

甘辛度
Sweet-dryness

甘 ——————— 辛
Sweet ——————— Dry

味わい
Taste

淡麗 ——————— 濃醇
Light ——————— Rich

香り
Aroma

低 ——————— 高
Weak ——————— Strong

蔵の創業は昭和48年 (1973)。地元の米で、地元の蔵人が醸す心安らぐ地酒だ。

The brewery was founded in Showa 48 (1973). Local-grown rice are used. It is a local sake makes you relax made by a local brewer.

原料米 トヨニシキ
酵母 協会901号　アルコール度数 5
日本酒度 −90 〜 −70　酸度 3.0 〜 4.0
精米分合 65%　小売価格 741円 300ml
Raw material rice: Toyonishiki
Yeast: Kyokai 901　Alcohol content: 5%
Sake meter value: -90--70
Acidity: 3.0-4.0
Rice-polishing rate: 65%
Retail price: 741yen/300ml

ICHINOKURA 一ノ蔵

所 〒 987-1393　宮城県大崎市松山千石字大欅 14 番地
☎ 0229-55-3322　酒蔵見学 可（要予約）
URL https://www.ichinokura.co.jp/
Add: 14 Matsuyama sengoku aza ookeyaki, Osaki-shi, Miyagi 987-1393　**Tel:** +81-229-55-3322　**Brewery tour:** YES (reservation required)　**URL:** http://www.ichinokura.co.jp/english

SAWANOI KIOKEJIKOMI IROHA

Wooden-bucket prepared sake / 澤乃井　木桶仕込　彩は

Tokyo／東京

蔵の敷地内の杉の木で仕込み桶を造り、昔ながらの生酛仕込みで醸した日本酒文化の伝統が詰まった純米酒。丸みのある旨みとしっかりとした酸味で、燗も旨い。

Using a traditional Kimoto starter culture, this revival sake is made gathering Japanese sake tradition and culture. It uses a large bucket which is made with a Japanese cedar grown in the brewery's property.

蔵の創業は元禄15年(1702)。奥多摩の秩父古生層の洞窟から湧き出る石清水で醸す酒には、川に棲む岩魚の塩焼きがおすすめ。

The brewery was founded in Genroku 15 (1702). Fresh water sprung from a cave of Chichibu Paleozoic formations in Okutama is used.

原料米 アケボノ
酵母 非公開　アルコール度数 15度以上16度未満　日本酒度 -1　酸度 2.2
精米分合 65%　小売価格 1650円 720ml
Raw material rice: Akebono
Yeast: Closed
Alcohol content: 15-15.9%
Sake meter value: -1　Acidity: 2.2
Rice-polishing rate: 65%
Retail price: 1650yen/720ml

OZAWA SHUZO　小澤酒造

所 〒198-0712　東京都青梅市沢井 2-770
☎ 0428-78-8210　酒蔵見学 可（詳細は電話かホームページにて。要予約）
URL http://www.sawanoi-sake.com/
Add: 2-770 Sawai, Ome-shi, Tokyo 198-0712　Tel: +81-428-78-8210　Brewery tour: YES (For details, call or see HP below. Reservation required)　URL: http://www.sawanoi-sake.com/

甘辛度
Sweet-dryness
甘　　　　　辛
Sweet　　　　Dry

味わい
Taste
淡麗　　　　濃醇
Light　　　　Rich

香り
Aroma
低　　　　　高
Weak　　　　Strong

HOW TO ENJOY SAKE

日本酒の楽しみ方

Enjoy Japanese sake at various temperatures

日本酒は温度で楽しむ

　日本酒はビールやワインなどと比べて、さまざま温度で楽しめるのも大きな特徴だ。また、右の表のように温度帯によって、香り、飲み口、味わいも変化する。例えば大吟醸や吟醸酒は、冷蔵庫で冷やして飲むのが一般的だ。冷蔵庫から取り出した時の温度は、「花冷え」と呼ばれる状態。果実のような吟醸香と、繊細な味わい、切れの良さが楽しめる。そして冷蔵庫から取り出してしばらく経った状態が「涼冷え（すずひえ）」だ。果実香が膨らみ、味わいにも甘さととろみが加わり、料理にも合う。また、純米酒や本醸造酒、普通酒は、冷やから燗まで楽しめるタイプが多い。なかでも酸が強い、しっかりした旨みがあるものは、飲んだ時に温かいと感じるぬる燗や、猪口を持つとやや熱さを感じる上燗あたりがおすすめで、さらに豊潤となる。

Compared to beer or wine, one notable feature of Japanese sake is enjoyable at various temperatures. Moreover, as the chart on the right shows, the aroma, texture and taste vary with the temperature. For example, Daiginjo and Ginjo-shu are commonly chilled in the refrigerator. The temperature when it is taken out of the refrigerator is called "Hanahie". You can enjoy fruity aroma, subtle taste and sharp aftertaste with Hanahie. The temperature it is taken out of the refrigerator and left at room temperature for a while is called "Suzuhie". Fruity aroma is enhanced, the taste gets sweeter and thicker and it matches with a meal. Many of Junmai-shu, Hon jozo-shu and non-premium sake are commonly enjoyable either chilled or warmed hot. Especially, for sake with high acidity and firm flavor, it is recommended to warm it to "Nurukan" the temperature you would feel it is warm by drinking or "Jokan" the temperature you would feel it is a little hot when you hold the choko (sake cup) since it would taste richer.

Example terms of temperatures for Japanese sake

日本酒を飲む温度の表現の例

Variation of taste by temperature
温度による味の変化

Chilled
冷やす

Warmed
温める

	Aroma 香り	
Being light (Closed) さわやかになる（閉じる）		**Being aromatic (Enhanced)** ふくよかになる（広がりがある）
	Texture 飲み口	
Being sharp (Crisp) すっきりとする（引き締まる）		**Being mild** まろやかになる
	Taste 味わい	
Sharp and feel dry 切れよく、ドライに感じる		**Sweetness and flavor are enhanced** 甘味、旨味成分が広がる

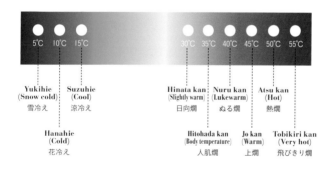

5℃　10℃　15℃　　　　30℃　35℃　40℃　45℃　50℃　55℃

Yukihie (Snow cold)
雪冷え

Suzuhie (Cool)
涼冷え

Hinata kan (Slightly warm)
日向燗

Nuru kan (Lukewarm)
ぬる燗

Atsu kan (Hot)
熱燗

Hanahie (Cold)
花冷え

Hitohada kan (Body temperature)
人肌燗

Jo kan (Warm)
上燗

Tobikiri kan (Very hot)
飛びきり燗

OKAN

御燗

燗酒は、秋冬に限らず一年中楽しめる飲み
方だ。温めることでさらに旨くなることを
「燗上がりする」という。純米酒や生酛・山
廃などの造りの酒は、酸や旨みが強いので
温めるとさらに味わいが深まり、脂の乗っ
た魚類や肉などとの相性も格段に増す。
温めるとやわらかい口当たりになるので、
酒器は飲み口がやや厚めの焼き物のぐい呑
みなどが合う。また、燗酒はアルコールの
吸収が早いのでいきなり酔いが回ることが
ない。身体に優しく酔えるのも安心だ。

You can enjoy warmed sake all year round, not only during fall
and winter. Enhancement of flavor by warming the sake is called
"Kan-agari". Pure-rice sake, unpasteurized sake and sake made
with Yamahai have strong sourness and flavor; therefore, the
taste gets deeper by warming up and matches even better with
marbled fish or meat dishes. The texture becomes mellow by
warming up, so a large pottery cup which has a thick edge is
suitable. Moreover, alcohol of warm sake is absorbed fast, so you
would not get drunk suddenly. You can feel good with sake without worrying too much about your health.

REISHU

冷酒

大吟醸酒や吟醸酒は、今や和食だけでは
なく、フレンチやイタリアンなどにも合う
酒として、世界中からも関心が高い。手間
と時間をかけて低温発酵で造られる吟醸造
りの酒は、香りや味わいが非常に繊細だ。
冷やしてワイングラスや薄手のガラス器に
注ぎ、格調高い調和のとれた味わいを楽し
もう。火入れをしていない生酒やしぼりた
ても、冷酒の方がフレッシュな味わいがそ
のまま楽しめる。1回火入れの生詰酒や生
貯蔵酒は、冷やして飲む夏酒の定番だ。

Today, Daiginjo-shu and Ginjo-shu attract much interest of people all over the world as a suitable sake matches with French and
Italian dishes, not only Japanese cuisine. Ginjo-zukuri sake made
by low temperature fermentation taking time and effort has very
subtle aroma and taste. Recommended to chill and pour it into a
wine glass or thin glass to enjoy the refined, balanced taste. Unpasteurized sake and freshly pressed sake without pasteurization
also taste good and fresh by reishu (chilled). Namazume-shu and
nama chozo-shu which are pasteurized once are often chilled
and enjoyed in summer.

The drinking vessels for sake
酒の器

日本酒の酒器には、伝統技術の粋を凝らした陶器や焼き物、塗り物、錫物、切子などさまざまな種類がある。最近では、日本酒のためにデザインされたワイン型のグラスなども登場している。さあ、お気に入りの酒器で楽しもう。

There are various kinds of the drinking vessel for sake — a pottery, lacquer ware, tin ware, cut glass and so on. Most of them are made with traditional sophisticated skills. In these days, some new vessels appear like a wine glass designed for sake. Enjoy sake with your favorite one!

KUTANI 九谷焼

KABURAKI SHOHO　鏑木商舗

九谷焼は江戸時代、加賀藩の殖産政策として始まった伝統的な色絵磁器で、多彩な色を駆使して描かれる。これは、美しい九谷焼を柄の部分に採用した、無鉛クリスタル製で、風味を引き立てるデザインの酒グラス。石川県金沢市で九谷焼窯元として代々続く鏑木商舗のオリジナル商品だ。酒グラス M 本金花詰2万2680円〜

Kutani is traditional porcelain decorated colorfully with a colored picture, which was encouraging by the Kaga Province in the Edo period. The glass of the photo is made from lead-free crystal and designed to emphasize the flavors of sake. Its beautiful pattern is painted by Kutani method. This is the original item made by Kaburagi Shoho that is a successive pottery producer of Kutani in Kanazawa, Ishikawa. Sake grass (M) Honkin Hanazume 22,680 yen ~

微細な青い粒で渦模様を描き、金を盛り上げて紋や唐草を配した酒盃。反った縁により、酒が優しく口に広がり旨みが引き立つ。酒杯 渦打青粒4万7520円

The drinking cup on which the spiral pattern is drawn with blue grains and some patterns like chinese arabesque are decorated with gold. It is gorgeously decorated with gold and flavors of sake spreads softly in the mouth with going over the curled edge of it. Shuhai Uzu-uchi Aochibu 47,500 yen ~

地の余白を余すことなく、器全体に九谷伝統の深い緑を鮮やかに塗る青手。口径の大きな酒盃 L は、香りも同時に楽しめるように。酒杯 L 青手雀7560円

The sake grass painted by Kutani method, the way of painting entirely with vivid and deep green color leaving no blank space. The cup L with larger lip is designed to enjoy flavor and aroma at the same moment. Shuhai (L) Aote-suzume 7,560 yen

赤い細やかな線の描写に金で彩りを加え、迫力と繊細さを兼ね備えた赤絵細描画。酒盃の縁の反りはそのままに、脚つきなので持ちやすい。高杯 赤絵細描龍4万1040円

This is the gorgeous Akae of power and delicacy, which is painted with detail red drawing and added color with gold. The edge of the glass is curved but it is easy to hold with a stem. Takahai Akae-saibyo Ryu 41,040 yen ~

器に張った銀箔の上に釉薬をかけて焼き上げた、銀のきらめきが美しいぐい呑み。筒形デザインは酒が辛口に感じ、燗も冷めにくい。銀彩水色4320円

The beautiful shot glass with silver sparkling, which is covered with silver leaf, grazed over it and baked up. The cylindrical shape makes dry flavor strong and keeps warmed sake cool off. Ginsai sky blue 4,320 yen ~

九谷焼の持ち手には繊細な雪の結晶、縁には結晶をモチーフにしたような幾何学模様が描かれて美しい。お酒をスッキリと楽しみたい時に。酒グラス S 雪の華金2万5920円~

This glass has beautiful snowflakes printed on its stem and a geometric pattern inspired by a snowflake on the edge of the base by Kutani method. This slender glass is good to enjoy refreshing taste. Sake glass (S) Yukino-hana Gold 25,920 yen ~

古九谷のうち、白地に鮮やかな色彩を描く「五彩手」と呼ばれる画風。ふっくらしたデザインは、まるみや甘さが膨らむ。酒グラス L 古九谷鳥文1万8360円~

This Kokutani is painted by the method of called Gosaide, which is to paint vivid colors on a white coat. Its round shape emphasizes a mellow and sweet taste of sake. Sake grass (L) Kokutani Tori-mon 18,360 yen ~

所 〒920-0865 石川県金沢市長町1丁目3-16　電076-221-6666　営9:00 ～ 22:00(日曜・祝日：～ 18:00)　休 不定休　URL http://kaburaki.jp/

Add: 1-3-16, Nagamachi, Kanazawa, Ishikawa, 920-0865　Tel: 076-221-6666　Hours:9:00-22:00(Sundays&Holidays-18:00)　Closed:Irregular Holidays　URL: http://kaburaki.jp/

GLASS ガラス

RIEDEL リーデル

260年以上の歴史を誇るオーストリアのワイン
グラスの老舗・リーデル社が、約8年の歳月を
かけて開発した純米酒の専用グラス。大ぶり
で横長、飲み口の口径が大きい形状が、純米
酒の特徴であるふくよかな米の旨み最大限に引
き出し、やわらかくクリーミーな質感を口の中
に長く留める。<エクストリーム>純米3000円。

A special glass for Junmai-shu that Riedel, the
long-running wine glass company which has a
history of over 260 yeas in Australia, has devel-
oped in about eight years time. The large and
wide shape with the large lip emphasizes a gorgeous flavor of rice which is characteristic of Junmai-shu to the maximum and keeps creamy texture long in a mouth. <Extreme> Junmai 3,000
yen

縦長のボウル形状が、瑞々しくフ
ルーティな香りや爽やかなのど越
しをもたらす大吟醸酒用グラス。<
リーデル・オー>大吟醸オー 2500円

A glass for Dai ginjo-shu. Its vertically
long and ball-like shape brings a
fresh fruity aroma and refreshing
feelings in passing the throat. <Rie-
del O> Daiginjo O 2,500 yen

蔵元とのワークショップを経て
2000年に発売された、大吟醸酒用
グラス。吟醸香がグラスの中で膨
らむのが特徴。<ヴィノム>大吟
醸4000円

A glass for Dai ginjo-shu released in
2000 after workshop with breweries. The aroma of ginjo increasing
in the glass is unique. <Vinum>
Daiginjo 4,000 yen

〒107-0062 東京都港区南青山青山1-1-1ツインタワー東館1F ☎03-
3404-4456 平日11:00〜20:00、土・祝10:00〜18:00 休日・年末年始
URL https://www.riedel.co.jp/　Add: East Building 1F, 1-1-1, Aoyama Twin
Tower, Minamiaoyama, Minato-ku, Tokyo, 107-0062　Tel: 03-3404-4456　Hou
rs:Weekday11:00~20:00,Saturdays&Holidays 10:00~18:00)　Closed:
Sundays&New Year's Holidays　URL: https://www.riedel.co.jp/

ARITA 有田焼

JTOPIA　ジェイトピア

全体に掛けられた漆黒の釉薬、黒い地に金銀が輝く斑紋が表れることから「油滴天目（ゆてきてんもく）」と呼ばれてきた。この戦国大名たちも愛した美しい焼き物を、長年に渡り追求し続けて完成したぐい呑み。深い藍と漆黒の斑紋は美しい銀河の輝きのようで、宇宙の神秘が酒にも宿る。口縁部には伝統的な技法で本金も施している。平天目型ぐい呑み　銀河本金彩1万2000円。（直径約8.8cm）

This is called Yuteki-tenmoku because it is soused entirely with pitch-dark glaze and glittering markings of gold and silver appear on its black coat. It has been completed after a long pursuing for this beautiful pottery loved by Japanese military commanders in the Sengoku period. The markings of deep indigo blue and pitch-dark look like a gloss of the beautiful galaxy and sake poured on them seems to contain the mysteries of the universe. The lip of the glass is decorated with gold, using traditional methods. Hiratenmoku sake cup Ginga Honkinsai 12,000 yen (diameter: about 8.8 cm)

天然の天草産天然陶石を用いた有田焼の極上磁器で、保温保湿性に優れ、冷酒・熱燗ともにおいしく飲める。桐箱入りで贈り物にも人気だ。

The premium Arita pottery made from natural pottery stone of Amakusa. It is excellent in moisture-retaining and warmth-keeping properties and both cold and warmed sake can be enjoyed with it. This glass is popular as a gift because it is placed in a paulownia box.

☎03-4405-6768（平日10:00 ～ 16:30）　🕐10:00 ～ 17:30　URL https://www.jtopia.co.jp/
Tel: 03-4405-6768 **URL:** https://www.jtopia.co.jp/

TSUGARUNURI 津軽塗

EBISUYA 恵比須屋

津軽塗とは、江戸時代から津軽地方（青森県）に伝わる伝統工芸
漆器。軽くて実用性に富み、優美な漆模様が特徴だ。写真の猪口
は、独特な斑点模様を持つ唐塗。この技法は漆を塗って、乾かし、
研ぐという作業を何度も繰り返し、全部で48の工程を経て2か月
近くかけて完成させる。呂上（茶）・赤上各4800円（直径5.5cm）

Tugarunuri is a traditional lacquer ware handed down in the Tsugaru
region of Aomori Prefecture from the Edo period. It is light and rich in
practicality and the characteristic of it is the exquisite lacquer pattern. The sake cup on the photo is Karanuri which has unique markings. Karanuri is the method that consists of 48 processes including
repeating operations of lacquering, drying and polishing over and
over. It takes nearly two months to complete all processes. Roage
(Brown)•Akaage 4,800 yen each (diameter: 5.5 cm)

〒030-0802　青森県青森市本町1-1-41
017-776-2116　平日9:00～18:00　休
毎月第2・第4日曜日　URL http://www.
ebisuyatsugarunuri.net　Add: 1-1-41,
Honcho, Aomori-shi, Aomori, 030-0802　Tel:
017-776-2116　Hours: 9:00-18:00　Closed:
Second Sunday&Fourth Sunday　URL: http://
www.ebisuyatsugarunuri.net

TIN 錫 （すず）

NOUSAKU 能作

富山県高岡市の伝統産業・鋳物の加工技術を
使って作られた、錫ならではのやわらかさと
温かみを感じるぐい呑みだ。錫100％のため
抗菌性に優れ、熱伝導率が高く、昔から水
を浄化し飲みものをまろやかにする作用もあ
るといわれている。冷酒を注ぐと、さらにお
いしく感じられる。Kuzushi-Yure-大 5000円
（直径約8cm前後）

This is a sake cup made with traditional casting
skills and techniques of Takaoka city in Toyama
Prefecture and it has warm touch and soft texture unique to tin. The product made of 100%
tin has excellent antibacterial effects and high
thermal conductivity. It is said that tin castings
has the effect of purifying water and making
drinks mellow and cold sake becomes more
flavorful after pouring into it.Kuzushi-
Yure(Big)5400yen (diameter: about8cm)

所 〒939-1119　富山県高岡市オフィスパーク8-1　本社FACTORY SHOP
☎0766-63-0002　営10:00 ～ 18:00　休年　末　年　始　URLhttp://www.
nousaku.co.jp/　**Add:** 8-1, Office Park, Takaoka-shi, Toyama, 939-1119　**Tel:**
0766-63-0002　**Hours:** 10:00-18:00　**Closed:**New Year's Holidays　**URL:** http://
www.nousaku.co.jp/

MASHIKO 益子焼　KOHIKI（粉引）（こひき）

WAKASAMA TOGEI　わかさま陶芸

粉引とは、成形した褐色の素地の上に白い
泥土をつけ、透明な釉薬をかけて焼いた陶
器で、朝鮮王朝時代に日本に伝来した。益
子焼にも粉引は多く、やわらかな温かみの
ある白さが人気だ。写真の益子焼の粉引は、
手仕事の面取りで形作られた陰影の美しさ
と、土の温もりが感じられるぐい呑み。粉
引　猪口900円（1個・直径約6.5cm前後）

Kohiki is the pottery which is baked after being covered with white mud and transparent
graze on brown molded groundwork. It was
introduced to Japan during the Korean Dy-
nasties period. Many of Mashiko belongs to
Kohiki and popular for the soft and warm
white color. One on the photo is a sake cup
giving a beautiful impression of shadow
shaped by handiwork chamfering and a warm
touch of clay.

所 〒321-4104　栃木県芳賀郡益子町大沢2271-9　☎0285-72-7414　営8:30 ～
17:30　休土・日・祝日　URLhttps://wakasama-mashiko.com/　**Add:** 2221-9,
Osawa, Mashikomachi, Haga-gun, Tochigi, 321-4104　**Tel:** 0285-72-7414　**Hours:**
8:30-17:30　**Closed:** Saturday, Sunday, Holiday　**URL:** https://wakasama-mashiko.
com/

Sweetness/Dryness of Japanese sake

日本酒の甘い辛い

　日本酒の「甘い辛い」の目安となるものに、日本酒度（酒度）と酸度がある。日本酒度は水の比重を±0としたときの、日本酒の比重を数値化したものだ。日本酒に糖分が多いと比重が重くなり、マイナスの数値で示される。反対に糖分が少ないと比重が軽くなり、プラスの数値で示される。つまりマイナスの数値が低いほど糖分が多いので甘く、プラスの数値が高いほどアルコール分が多いので辛く感じるというわけだ。酸度は日本酒に含まれる乳酸やコハク酸など、有機酸の量を表したもの。同じ日本酒度だと、酸度が高い方が辛く濃く、少ない方が甘く淡麗に感じられる。

"Sweetness/Dryness" of Japanese sake are measured by Sake meter value and Acidity. Sake meter value indicates a specific gravity of Japanese sake by setting the gravity of water as ±0. When sake has a high sugar content, the gravity is heavier and is indicated as − (minus). When sake has a low sugar content, the gravity is lighter and is indicated as + (plus). It means, - means sweet because it has a high sugar content and + means dry because it has more alcohol content. Acidity indicates amounts of organic acids such as lactic acid and succinic acid contained in sake. When compared sake with the same sake meter value, sake with a higher acidity tastes dry and rich. Sake with a lower acidity tastes sweet and light.

LET'S GO TO IZAKAYA

居酒屋へ行く

兵庫県 櫻正宗 600円
山形県 出羽桜 吟醸酒 600円
埼玉県 花陽浴 (ハナアビ) 800円
岩手県 あづまみね 純米吟醸 鶴 900円
宮城県 乾坤一 (けんこんいち) 純米吟醸 650円
石川県 菊姫 500円

新潟県 加茂錦 純米大吟醸 荷札酒 650円
群馬県 町田酒造 特伝限定 600円
福島県 奈良萬 純米 600円
栃木県 若駒 600円
新潟県 たかちよ 限定 純米 650円
福島県 廣戸川 特別純米 600円

富山県 満寿泉 ますいずみ 400円
新潟県 〆張鶴 本醸造 月 420円
宮城県 あたごのまつ 辛口 450円
石川県 手取川 辛口 山廃本醸 450円
富山県 成政 足番辛口 500円
鹿児島県 吉兆宝山 芋焼酎 500円

長崎県 ちんぐ 壱岐麦焼酎 500円
鯛ビハ 400円
おつまみ 400〜450円
腰古井 辛口 ¥400

What is IZAKAYA?

日本の居酒屋とは

　おいしい日本酒と、酒に合うおつまみが揃い、手頃な値段で気軽に楽しめるのが居酒屋の魅力だ。日本酒は、一年を通じて発売される定番タイプのほか、四季折々の季節で発売される、風味豊かな限定酒も多い。居酒屋に行くと、酒の種類を紙に書いて張り出している店もあるので、一杯目は定番タイプ、二杯目はその季節ならではの限定酒という風にして楽しむのもいい。そして、つまみに関しても全く同じだ。定番のおつまみから、季節ならではの旬の魚介や山の幸、日本各地の珍味まである。日本酒は幅広い料理に合うので失敗は少ない。気軽に日本酒とつまみのマリアージュを楽しもう。

The charm of Izakaya, a Japanese gastropub, is that they provide delicious sakes and nibbles matching to it at reasonable prices and people enjoy drinking comfortably. Some sakes are basic drinks sold throughout a year, while others are limited seasonal items that have rich flavors. At Izakaya, you can find the menu of sake stuck over the wall and choose which one you drink. For example, to enjoy a basic one at first and next order a seasonal one. The same was true with nibbles. There are various kinds of nibbles from basic dishes and delicious seasonal food from the mountains and the sea to the delicacies of all the places of Japan. It is unlikely that you make a wrong choice because sake matches various kinds of dish. Take it easy and enjoy the mariage of sakes and nibbles!

Manners&HOW TO Visit

居酒屋のマナーと訪れ方

居酒屋は個室スタイルではなく、オープンスペースの場合が多い。知らない客と相席になった場合は、軽く挨拶しよう。また注文ごとの現金払いや、靴を脱ぐこともあるので、店のルールを確認しよう。

Most of izakaya don't have any private room. If you share a table with other visiters, you should say hi. Check the rule of the bar, such as which you should pay cash or charge and which you have to take off your shoes or not, because they are different depending on the bar.

Enjoy drinking in a good manner

マナーを守って楽しく飲もう

POINT 1

Not talking loudly. Some customers really enjoy drinking alone.

一人客も多いので大声を出すのはやめよう。

POINT 2

Avoid strong perfume because the seat is close to the next.

隣同士が近いので、強い香水はやめよう。

POINT 3

When you call a server, say 'Oniisan' to men or 'Oneesan' to women.

店員を呼ぶときは男性なら「お兄さん」、女性なら「お姉さん」と呼ぼう

Useful phrases in izakaya

居酒屋で役立つ言葉

PHRASE
(1)

"Do you have a table for ◯?"

◯人ですが、入れますか？

◯nindesu ga hairemasuka?

PHRASE
(2)

"Excuse me. May I see a menu, please?"

すみません、メニューを見せてください。

Sumimasen, Menu wo misete kudasai.

PHRASE
(3)

"What is today's special sake and nibbles?"

今日のおすすめの日本酒とおつまみは何ですか？

Kyou no osusume no nihon-shu to otsumami ha nandesuka?

PHRASE
(4)

"Which sake do you recommend as the second?"

2杯目の日本酒は何がいいですか？

Nihaime no nihon-shu ha nani ga iidesuka?

PHRASE
(5)

"Which food do you recommend to finish off drinking"

おすすめの、しめの食事を教えてください。

Osusume no shime no shokuji wo oshiete kudasai.

PHRASE
(6)

"Thank you for the wonderful meal. Can I have my check, please?"

ごちそうさまでした。お会計お願いします。

Gochisousama deshita. Okaikei onegai shimasu.

Izakaya Menu

居酒屋のメニュー

居酒屋の料理は、単品メニューがほとんどだ。一人客も多いので1品の量は少なめだが、その分たくさんの種類の料理が楽しめる。居酒屋の代表的な人気メニューを知っておこう。

Most of the dish provided at izakaya is a single item. They are small portions for solo-drinker so you can enjoy many kinds of dishes. This page introduces popular menus of Izakaya.

Sashimi [slices of raw seafood]

刺身

新鮮な魚介類を生のまま切り、醤油やワサビなどをつけて食べる料理。季節によって獲れる魚介が違うので、旬の魚も味わえる。

The dish made by cutting fresh raw seafood and eaten with soy sauce, wasabi and so on. You can enjoy seasonal tastes because kinds of seafood vary with seasons.

Otoshi [special appetizer]
お通し

酒を頼むと一緒に出てくる、店のおすすめ料理（有料）。出ない店もある。写真はキュウリとワカメ（海藻）の酢の物。

This is part of the service charge, which is recommended food provided with sake of your order. Some izakaya don't have it. The photo is a vinegared dish of seaweed, cucumbers and bamboo shaped fish past cake.

| Column |

Sakizuke [appetizer]
先付

すぐできる簡単な小料理。居酒屋は客が多いので、メイン料理に時間がかかるときなどに注文する。

A simple dish which can be ready in a minute. Many costumers come to izakaya so they order this kind of dishes when it takes time to ready a main dish.

Salad
サラダ

居酒屋のサラダは、ジャガイモをつぶしてマヨネーズで和えたポテトサラダが定番。マカロニサラダも人気がある。

Potato salad is the basic menu of izakaya made with mashed potato and mayonnaise. Macaroni salad is also popular.

Kushiyaki [spit-roasting]
串焼き

鶏肉、豚肉、牛肉、野菜などを串に刺して、タレを付けて焼いた料理。好きなものを1本ずつ注文できる。

A cookery that is made by sticking pieces of chicken, pork, beef and vegetables and roasting them with some sauce. You can order one stick.

Grill dish
焼き物

魚の干物や切り身を焼き、醤油と大根
おろしなどで食べる料理。日本酒の燗
酒などとの相性は抜群だ。

This dish that dried fish or fish fillet are
grilled is eaten with soy sauce and grated
daikon radish. It especially marries with
warmed sake.

Fritter
揚げ物

写真のイカや、タコ、小魚などに衣を
つけて油で揚げた料理。好みでレモン
や塩などを振りかけて食べる。

As the photo, this is the dish made by frying
squid, octopus, small fish and so on in bat-
ter. It is eaten with lemon juice or salt.

Stewed dishes
煮物

豚や牛のホルモンを味噌や醤油の汁で
煮込んだ、居酒屋の定番料理。辛口の
本醸造酒や普通酒に合う。

A basic menu of izakaya that stewed inter-
nal organs of pork or beef with miso or soy
soup. It matches to dry Honjozo-shu and
Futsu-shu.

Meal
食事

居酒屋で飲んだあと、最後のしめには、
写真の明太子のお茶漬けなど、お腹が
落ち着くご飯ものや麺が人気だ。

Rice or noodle dishes make you modestly
full like mentai chazuke on the photo are
popular to end up drinking at izakaya,

RESTAURANTS SERVING SAKE IN TOKYO

東京で日本酒が飲める店

日本酒バーをコンセプトにしてオープン。スタイリッシュな店内は照明も落としてあり、大人の雰囲気が漂う。カウンター前のガラス張りの大型冷蔵庫には、全国各地の日本酒の一升瓶がずらりと並ぶ。酒肴も全国から取り寄せた珍味や旬の魚介、銘柄鶏豚など、こだわりの和物がずらりと並ぶ。

This bar was open as a Japanese sake bar. A stylish interior and dimming lights create a mature atmosphere. In the showcase type refrigerator in front of the counter, there are a lot of sake bottles from various places of Japan. You can also enjoy selected Japanese nibbles such as delicacies from all parts of Japan, seasonal seafood, branded chicken and pork and so on.

写真のホタルイカの塩辛やホヤの塩漬け、カズノコくんせいなど、全国各地から取り寄せる珍味は約20種類。なかなか手に入らないものが多く、日本酒にも抜群に合うので、これ目当ての客も多い。日本酒は写真の60mlのショットグラスから注文できる。

There are about 20 kinds of delicacies which is ordered from all over Japan such as fermented product of firefly squid salted sea squirt, smoked herring roe on the photo, and so on. Most of them are rare and many customers aim at these foods. Sake can be ordered from a shot glass of 60ml.

日本酒は一升瓶で約50種類が冷蔵庫に揃う。すべて全国各地の違う銘柄で構成され、無くなるとさらに違う銘柄が並ぶ。季節限定酒も含めると、年間で約2000種類もの日本酒を扱うという。昔スタイルのお燗器もある。

About 50 kinds of 1 -sho sake bottle always line up in the refrigerator. Each bottle is a different brand and they replenish stock with another one when any brand runs out. The bar handles about 2,000 kinds of sake in a year including limited seasonal brand and have an old-fashioned sake warmer.

Shop DATA

所〒105-0004 東京都港区新橋3-19-4桜井ビル2F ☎03-3438-3375 営月〜金17：00〜24：00（LO肴23：00 飲み物23：30）土16：00〜24：00（LO肴23：00 飲み物23：30）休日祝 ¥約3500円〜

Add: Sakurai Building 2F, 3-19-4, Shinbashi, Minato-ku, Tokyo, 105-0004 **Tel:** 03-3438-3375 **Hours:** [weekday]17:00-24:00 (LO.Food 23:00/Drink 23:30) [Sat]16:00-24:00 (LO.Food 23:00/Drink 23:30) **Closed:** Sun, Holidays **Budget:** about 3,500 yen

standing room SUZUDEN

スタンディングルーム鈴傳

Shop DATA

所 〒160-0004　東京都新宿区四谷1-10　電03-3351-1777　営
平日17：00～21：00　休土日祝　お盆　年始年末　予約
2000円～

Add: 1-10, Yotsuya, Shinjuku-ku, Tokyo, 160-0004　Tel: 03-3351-1777　Hours: 17:00-21:00　Closed: Sat, Sun; Holidays, Bon, Year-end and New Year　Budget: about 2,000 yen -

江戸時代から続く老舗酒屋にある立ち飲み酒場。酒屋の一角で酒を飲ませることを「角打ち」というが、東京での草分け的存在だ。日本酒は常時20種類くらいあり、季節により7～8種類が入れ替わる。金曜日は「十四代」の日で、幻の酒が安く飲める。20種類ほどのつまみは家庭料理が中心ですべて手作り。酒もつまみも注文時に現金で払う。店内のレトロな風情も酒肴にしよう。

The standing bar in the long-running liquor store established in the Edo period. Providing sake on the corner of a liquor store is called Kakuuchi and this bar is its pioneer of Tokyo. They always handle about 20 kinds of sake and 7-8 kinds of them are replaced seasonally. Friday is 'Juyondai' Day and this phantom sake is provided at a reasonable price. About 20 kinds of nibbles are mainly homemade dishes and all handmade. You have to pay cash when you order some food or drink. Enjoy drinking with retro atmosphere.

SAKENODAIMASU
KAMINARIMONTEN

酒の大桝 雷門店

Shop DATA

雷門すぐ前の、酒屋の奥に店がある。定番品や季節商品を合わせ、常時120種類の日本酒が揃い、90mlから注文できる。浅草神社のお神酒は店が監修しており、酒米の王者・山田錦を使ったおいしい本醸造酒。参拝記念の一杯としても大人気だ。つまみは手づくりのものなど多彩だが、クリームチーズの味噌漬けはファンが多い。干しホタルイカの炙りは燗酒に合う。

所 〒111-0032　東京都台東区浅草1-2-8　☎03-5806-3811　営 平日：16:00〜23:30　土日祝12:00〜23:30　休 火曜（祝日の場合は翌日）　予 約2000円〜

Add: 1-2-8, Asakusa, Taito-ku, Tokyo, 111-0032　Tel: 03-5806-3811　Hours: [Weekday] 16:00-23:30 [Sat, Sun, Holiday] 12:00-23:30　Closed: Tue (Wednesday is closed in the week when Tuesday is holiday)　Budget: about 2,000 yen -

The bar is at the back of a liquor store, located in front of Kaminari-mon Gate. They always handle 120 kinds of sake including basic items and seasonal ones and you can order from 90ml. The sacred sake of Asakusa-jinja Shrine which the bar supervises is delicious Honjozo-shu made from Yamadanishiki, the king rice for sake. It is popular as a memory of visiting. They have various nibbles. The cream cheese pickled in miso has many fans and the grilled dried-firefly-squid matches warmed sake.

SAKAGURA RESTAURANT TAKARA

酒蔵レストラン 宝

Shop DATA

 〒100-0005 東京都千代田区丸の内3-5-1 東京国際フォーラム B1 ☎03-5223-9888 月〜金11：30〜14：00 17：00〜23：00 土日祝11：30〜15：30 17：00〜22：00 無休（年末年始除く） 約4000円〜

Add: Tokyo International Forum B1, 3-5-1, Marunouchi, Chiyoda-ku, Tokyo, 100-0005 Tel:03-5223-9888 Hours: [Weekday] 11:30-14:00, 17:00-23:00 [Sat, Sun, Holidays] 11:30-15:30, 17:00-22:00 Closed: Only Year-end and New year holiday Budget: about 4,000 yen-

有楽町の東京国際フォーラムのB1にあるので外国人客も多い。運営パートナーとして参加する9蔵の日本酒を扱う。各蔵から直送されるしぼりたてや冷やおろしなどの季節商品や、ここでしか飲めない酒蔵渾身の純米大吟醸などもある。猪口に30mlずつ入った9蔵すべての日本酒が試せる、飲み比べセットも人気だ。酒蔵各地の名物食材を使った郷土料理を始め、カニ肉9割コロッケや一人軍鶏鍋などユニークなメニューも多い。

This is located at B1 of Tokyo International Forum in Yuraku-cho and a lot of foreigners visit there. They handle sakes of nine breweries which are business partners. You can enjoy seasonal bottles such as Shiboritate and Hiyaoroshi directly from the breweries and specially made Junmai Dai-ginjo which can only drink here. A sake fight menu of nine breweries in little cups is popular. They have a lot of unique menu — local cuisine made with special food of where breweries are, a croquette made from 90 % crab meat, Shamo-nabe (Japanese hotpot of fighting cock) and so on.

TESHIGOTOYA SEIGETSU

てしごとや 霽月

料理の様子が楽しめる、オープンキッチンスタイルの店だ。日本全国47都道府県の日本酒がすべて揃い、季節の酒などを含めると約100種類の日本酒が味わえる。料理は毎朝築地の市場で買い付ける新鮮な魚介や肉塊、野菜などを串に刺して炭火で焼く炉端スタイルが人気で、毎日メニューも変わる。外国人対応が可能なスタッフもいる。

This restaurant was open with an open kitchen where costumers can enjoy seeing that chefs are cooking. They handle sakes from all of forty-seven prefectures in Japan and you can enjoy about 100 kinds of sake including seasonal ones. The popular food menu is a type of Japanese barbecue-style 'robata-yaki', that spitted food like fresh seafood, meat and vegetables was burned in a charcoal fire. These ingredients are bought at the Tsukiji market every morning. Their menu varies from day to day. Some staffs can speak foreign languages.

Shop DATA

所 〒162-0825 東京都新宿区神楽坂 6-77 神谷ビル 2F 電 03-3269-4320 営 月〜木・土 17:00 〜 23:30 (LO22:30) 金 17:00〜翌 2:00 (LO1:00) 日・祝 17:00 〜 23:00 (LO22:00) 休 無休 予 約4500円〜

Add: Kamiya Building 2F, 6-77, Kagurazaka, Shinjuku-ku, Tokyo, 162-0825 Tel: 03-3269-4320 Hours: [Mon-Thu, Sat] 17:00-23:30 (LO, 22:30) [Fri] 17:00-2:00 (LO, 1:00) [Sun, Holiday] 17:00-23:00 (LO, 22:00) Closed: Nothing Budget: about 4,500 yen

SAKE WORDS

用語集

KAKEMAI

掛け米

醪（もろみ）を仕込むときに加える蒸し米。

Steamed rice used for mash fermenting.

- -

KANJIKOMI/KANZUKURI

寒仕込み／寒造り

酒造りに適した厳冬期（11〜3月ごろ）に行われる仕込みをさす。

The preparation which is done in a season of severe cold, from November to May.

- -

KIKIZAKE [sake tasting]

利き酒

酒の色や透明度、香り、味を識別し、総合的に分析する。

The total evaluating of the sake quality such as its color, clearness, aroma and taste.

- -

KOUJI

麹

蒸し米に麹カビを繁殖させたもの。米のデンプンを糖化させる役割がある。

The material that aspeigillus oryzae proliferates on steamed rice. It saccharifys the starch of rice to sugar.

- -

KOUBO [yeast]

酵母

糖分をアルコールに変える働きをする単細胞微生物。清酒の風味、香味をつくり出す。

A unicellular microorganism which converts sugar to alcohol. It makes the aroma and flavor of sake.

SHUBO [fermentation starter]

酒母

蒸し米、米麹、水に酵母を加え、大量に培養・増殖させたもの。醪のもとになる。

The yeast which is cultured in large quantities with steamed rice, koji and water. It is base of moromi.

DAKUSHU

濁酒

もろみを濾さない白くにごった酒で、どぶろくともいう。にごり酒は濾す工程が入るので清酒である。

Dakushu is a cloudy sake which is not filtered and called Doburoku. On the other hand, Nigorizake is classified to Seishu because it is filtered roughly.

TARUZAKE [cask sake]

樽酒

主に杉の樽で貯蔵された酒。木の香りが移り、独特の味わいがある。

Sake stored in a barrel mainly made of Japan cedar wood. It has a unique permeated flavor of wood.

MOROMI [fermentation mash]

醪 (もろみ)

酒母、蒸し米、麹、仕込み水を混ぜアルコール発酵させたもの。

A material that is alcohol-fermented by mixing shubo, steamed rice, koji and water.

YAWARAGIMIZU [chaser]

和らぎ水

日本酒を飲む合間に飲用する水をさす。悪酔いを防ぐ効果もある。

The action of gulping water from time to time while drinking sake. It has a preventing effect for drunken sickness.

CONCLUSION

おわりに

　今、日本酒は長い歴史を有しながらも日進月歩で進化する酒造技術や、和食以外も受け容れながら変化する私たちの嗜好を反映させ、多種多様な酒質が展開されています。近年海外で人気を呼んでいるのも、さまざまな料理に合うまったく新しい感覚の食中酒として、高い評価を得ているからといえるでしょう。本書では、製造方法や地域の食文化の違いに由来する酒質のバラエティーを、現代的なトレンドを交えながら紹介し、酒器や居酒屋の代表的な料理など酒の周辺文化にまつわる、伝統的な要素も取り上げながら、日本酒の持つ深く広い魅力をコンパクトに表わすことを心がけました。"古いようで、実は新しい酒"である日本酒を楽しむ上で、参考になれば幸いです。　松崎　晴雄

Today, with its long history, various types of Japanese sake are produced to reflect our preference in tastes to enjoy meals other than Japanese food, by rapidly advancing sake-making technologies. A popularity of sake overseas in recent years must be because it is highly regarded as a new genre of alcohol beverage which matches with many types of meals. I tried to express the deep and wide charms of Japanese sake as compact as possible by introducing a variety of sake comes from the differences of brewing methods and regional food cultures with recent trends referring traditional cultures related to sake such as drinking vessels and popular dishes served at Izakaya. I hope this book helps you to enjoy Japanese sake which "seems old but actually new".　Haruo Matsuzaki

松崎 晴雄（まつざき・はるお）

1960年神奈川県横浜市生まれ。上智大学外国語学部卒。株式会社西武百貨店に入社。商品部バイヤーや食品・和洋酒部門を担当。1997年、退社。現在、日本酒輸出協会（SEA）会長。『新版あなたの好みで味わうおいしい日本酒ガイド』『大人の探検・日本酒』（有楽出版社発行、実業之日本社販売）など著書多数。

Designer・DTP	佐々木志帆（ナイスク naisg.com） 沖増岳二
Editor	松尾里央、岸正章、柴田由美、河野将（ナイスク naisg.com）
Edit Cooperation	田中宏幸
Illustrator	山口正児
Translator	石田康衣、亀濱香
Photographer	中川文作
Special Thanks	小澤酒造、秋鹿酒造

the SAKE BOOK
日本酒ガイドブック《英語対訳つき》

2018年7月20日 初版第1刷発行

著者	松崎晴雄
発行者	岩野裕一
発行所	株式会社実業之日本社 〒153-0044　東京都目黒区大橋1-5-1　クロスエアタワー 8階 ［編集］電話　03-6809-0452 ［販売］電話　03-6809-0495 ［URL］http://www.j-n.co.jp/

印刷・製本 大日本印刷株式会社